Will Can You Help Me Create the Future Today?

A Guide To Making It Happen...

by

John R. Eggers

D.O.K. Publishers, P.O. Box 605, East Aurora, N.Y. 14052

This book is dedicated to my parents, Edgar and Helen Eggers of Waterville, Minnesota, who taught me by their example to cherish my heritage and thoroughly enjoy today. Without this firm hold on yesterday and today, without their constant support and confidence in me, the courage or desire to grapple with the future could never have been realized.

To increase the usefulness of this book, a duplicate set of activity and worksheet pages are provided. With permission granted, these pages appearing in the back of the book may be detached for photocopying or other means of reproduction.

ISBN No. 0-914634-84-4

© 1985
D.O.K. PUBLISHERS
EAST AURORA, NY 14052

CONTENTS

PREFACE

"How can I think about the future when I'm too busy solving yesterday's problems?"

This remark, made to me by an educator from Chicago, depicts the attitude of most educators concerning the importance of the future. I'm convinced, however, that less of "yesterday's problems" would exist if educators would consider where they need to go and how they are going to get there. To do this, one has to look ahead rather than behind.

Because education has not taken the time to adequately address what it is doing in terms of helping students live in the future, most of what is taught in today's schools could be classified as low priority because most of what is taught relates to living in the 1950's rather than 1980. And, of major importance, most of what is taught has little relevance for living beyond the 1980's. This book is intended to help teachers teach what is most important, namely-(1) to help students better understand their future and (2) to help students cope with their future today.

With educational change occurring at a snail's pace and with societal changes making quantum leaps, is there hope?

In spite of the above negative critique of today's schools, I am optimistic about schools and their ability to meet the challenges confronting them. Were it not for this optimism, the time and effort taken to write this book would have been better spent fishing in northern Minnesota.

My reason for optimism rests with today's teachers and their continued do or die efforts to make a difference in the lives of their students. Schools don't make the difference, teachers in the classroom make the difference. For this reason, this book is intended for teachers who are concerned about helping their students meet the demands of the future. This really is what schooling is all about but I'm convinced that schools can and must do a better job of assuring that today's students do possess the skills to create their own future. After all, the future is the place today's elementary and secondary students will be spending the rest of their lives.

Will teachers have to start all over again?

This book is not intended to be used as a separate course of study. It is not intended to replace what is already being taught, and it is not intended to merely serve as a supplement to what is now taught. Rather, the material is intended to be integrated, woven into current content, to futurize, if you will, what is now taught. Thus, teachers need not have to find special time to implement the material in this book.

What is so special about the material presented in this book?

The contents are special in a number of ways. It is student activity oriented, it is a "how to" book. Activities are intended to be presented "Monday morning", activities are intended to help students become aware of the future (if schools did nothing else, helping to make the future more real would be a giant step forward because through greater awareness comes a confidence to deal with the future), and each activity has a skill woven into it which is intended to help students cope with and excel in their future.

By giving emphasis to the activities and skills contained in this book, can teachers be assured that their students will be able to cope with what the future has in store?

Certainly by providing opportunities to become more aware of the future, students will have greater confidence in their abilities to deal with change. Considering the skills woven into the activities, I feel confident that the skills are more appropriate for dealing with the future than current curricular priorities. However, the nature in which these futuristic skills are presented, allows teachers to deal with both simultaneously -- thereby teaching old stuff a new way. Also, test scores measuring antiquated processes common in today's schools should not suffer because no radical departure from traditional content need be made.

With so much emphasis on the future, should the past be forgotten?

Much good was accomplished in the past and much can be learned from past mistakes. Thus, to re-invent the wheel would be as erroneous as the current practice of disregarding the future. To maintain a hold on the past while we grapple with the future, the illustrations in the book are taken from early history texts and school readers to serve as a reminder of the past.

Will this book make a difference?

No, this book alone will not make a difference. As was stated earlier, teachers make the difference in the lives of their students. They control the answer to this question. However, I firmly and confidently believe the chance will be greater for making a difference in the lives of students by implementing the activities contained herein. It is my sincere hope that this will occur.

John R. Eggers

ACKNOWLEDGMENTS

Certainly, acknowledgement pages have to be one of the least effective ways of paying tribute to people who have been influential in helping someone to successfully fulfill a major task. I often wonder what people do who do not write books to recognize the influence of others. Hopefully, they have chosen a more meaningful way to do what I am about to do.

Of course, having a son, John-Carlos (5) and two nieces, Kim (13) and Kelly Eggers (9), provide a special purpose for this book. No doubt, the felt need for writing would not have been as great if it were not for them. The book may even have gone unwritten.

Dr. Ron Barnes of Transitions, Inc. in Phoenix, Arizona, Dr. Harold Shane of Indiana University, and Ms. Cece Logan of the Collegiate Association for the Development and Renewal of Educators in Denver, Colorado and the Scenario advisory board members (Sister Judy Bisignano, Dr. Ron Burgo, Penny Damlo, Dr. Richard Dougherty, Robert Ferguson, Dr. Geoffrey Fletcher, Cindy Guy, Robert Hoffman, Bill Leikam, and Dr. Gary Wooddell) have given me their friendship and have enthusiastically supported my futures related endeavors. Their commitment to good schools and good teachers and continued support and friendship provide me the optimism and confidence to believe the best years in education are yet to come.

Marie Conlon of Denver, Colorado and Dr. Dave Mathias of Loveland, Colorado have achieved what all educators hope to achieve - namely to make a difference in the lives of students. Their past and present exemplary practice of teaching excellence continue to serve as an inspiration to me. Their confidence in me during my "awakening" years was especially important.

No other person is more responsible for lighting the path I took in education than Dr. Don Glines of the California State Department of Education. He took a risk one day in the Spring of 1972 when he hired me sight unseen from a teaching position in Tehran, Iran to teach at the Wilson Campus School in Mankato, Minnesota. The continual influence in my life via his accomplishments and efforts in pioneering new and significant paths in educational futures serve as guideposts for me and for many other educators.

If this book were to have a co-author, it would be Dr. Edward Pino of Parker, Colorado. Under Ed's tutelage, many of the concepts serving as the foundation for this book began to form. Dr. Pino's achievements as an educator are surpassed by few. Like Glines, he began pioneering futuristics programs years before educators began to realize the significance of futuristics upon education. The futures awareness growth of students as a result of using this book will be partially due to Dr. Pino's influence upon its writing.

Many people make sacrifices so that books can be written. No greater sacrifice was made than by Kathy, my wife. Were it not for her help as critic, proof reader, and typist, the book would not have reached a finality. All of this was done while being a mother, managing a house and an antique shop. Any thanks or appreciation given to me for writing this book goes also to you, Kathy.

FOREWORD

Mankind may be witnessing the beginning of the greatest global transformation in history, according to the majority of individuals currently analyzing future trends. If they prove correct, the present societal transitions will lead to the creation of a very different Twenty-First Century.

Federal, state, private, and community institutions will all be affected. Alfred Rock, predicting the future of post-secondary learning, stated: "Institutions of higher education in 1995 will not look like those we see today. They will be different in ways that will be startling, particularly considering the almost unchanging nature of these institutions in the last century."

The same thought can be applied to K-12 school districts. The issue is not whether the date may be 1995, or 1991, or 2004; the significant factor is that most all futurists indicate that schools as they now exist can not and will not remain the same as the new century approaches. Technological, biological, and social conditions promise to move education away from the schooling/work ethic values of the Twentieth Century Industrial Age, toward life long learning society for a New Age.

John Eggers, realizing the probable changes ahead, has provided an invaluable service for educators by creating a book designed to assist them through the eighties and beyond. If education must be significantly different, how can teachers begin the process of reform when the current tide has been calling for more and better basics, higher test scores, more stringent conventional requirements, proficiency and competency evaluations, and court-ordered desegregation, all in the face of declining enrollments, budget cuts, and ethnic population shifts?

John responds with practical, reality-oriented concrete suggestions that can be utilized in most any school now within present budgets, laws, and politics. His use of historical illustrations helps to bridge the gap between past, present, and future. His theme of "teaching old stuff in a new way" stresses that teachers can weave into the present curriculum and conpetencies requirements the concerns of the future. He illustrates how it can be accomplished by following the often stated advice of one of the great educators of America, Dr. Lloyd Trump, who repeatedly has told the profession that "improving existing schools is basically a matter of learning to do better with what you have." Will You Help Me Create the Future Today, by following the Trump approach, is a major contribution toward the effort to incorporate futures studies into the classroom.

This book is especially timely. Futures publications of the past years have primarily been by social scientists, scientists, ecologists, technologists - people specializing in food, population, economics, energy, oceans, space, lifestyles, electronics, and prolongevity, among others. Few educators have written about the future. When they have it has most often been in general terms related to projected changes in education, and has more often been developed for administrator and school board audiences, and secondary social studies courses.

Very little has been specifically prepared for elementary classroom teachers and their daily work with students. When participating in educational futures workshops, school and district staffs have repeatedly asked for lists of recommended books and materials that would help them right now - tomorrow afternoon - to assist younger students in their understanding of and visions of the potential personal and societal futures which might confront them in the eighties and nineties, and the longer range possibilities for the early decades of the next century.

The common response to such requests has been to recommend that teachers read several of the global and educational futures books; write for reproduced "handouts" from the few districts already involved in futures studies; subscribe to a few futures-oriented magazines; and develop local teacher-constructed materials. This advice has often led to time-consuming, frustrating experiences. With the pressing demand for basics, and the daily criticisms placed upon teachers, most have chosen not to try to create new "home-made" or school-level curriculum approaches.

Will You Help Me Create the Future Today changes all that. This book provides immediate how-to-do-it activities which can be integrated into existing classroom units. The highlight of the volume is the exciting Part V, which details fifty-one student classroom activities, involving six key processes, and important content for the future. That section is followed by "102 Futuristic Starter Ideas," which greatly expand the imagination capabilities of the many good creative teachers in education.

John Eggers deserves congratulations and thanks from educators every-where. This valuable volume, written in the spirit of the First Global Conference on the Future, will assist teachers in their efforts to help the students of today prepare to create tomorrow a preferable future for humankind and the biosphere.

Don E. Glines
Sacramento, California
August, 1980

PART I

Challenging Encounters Of An Endangered Kind: Today's Schools

Meeting Our Future: Are We Ready?

Not too long ago, my family was involved in a court hearing held in the judge's chambers to finalize the adoption of our son. Prior to going in to the judge's chambers, our four year old boy hopped off the bench where he was anxiously waiting and said quite profoundly, "I don't think I'm ready for this yet." Well he was ready, the hearing proceeded as planned and he is legally ours.

Interestingly, however, everyone today seems to be concerned about their inability or ability to be ready. At the global level, countries are spending much time and monies to be ready for the eventual depletion of oil. At the national level, a continuous debate occurs over a country's readiness to withstand any threat to world peace. A criteria for getting a job rests on a person's ability to be ready, to be prepared. Without a doubt, the degree of readiness has much to do with success whether it be a country, community or citizen. In relating readiness to education, one could conclude that boards of education grant readiness diplomas each year at high school graduation symbolizing the student has acquired the necessary skills to be ready for life.

Recently, public education has been challenged as to the credibility of these diplomas. Right or wrong, the questions of whether or not students are prepared to meet the challenges of today's and tomorrow's world is a valid question and certainly one that needs to be continually addressed by educators at all levels.

Why? Consider the time line of a child entering kindergarten today. He or she will be approximately twenty or twenty-five years old around the year 2000 and considering the longevity of men and women, he or she will probably be living around the year 2050. This means that they will be spending two thirds of their lives in the twenty-first century. If as many changes occur during the next seventy-five years as they have in the past seventy-five years or even in the past 10 years, it would seem the greatest challenge facing education is helping youth adapt to and live in this world yet to be discovered (i.e., the future).

There are many signs already indicating the future has begun to creep into the present. Cases in point: The "six million dollar man" has arrived in the form of pacemakers, intelligence pills, and artificial arteries. The science fiction world of Buck Rogers is no longer science fiction when considering the quantum leap made from the depths of the oceans to the heights of outer space. Orewell's 1984 is just around the corner but there are many indications that the world of 1984 was around 5 years ago if not earlier. Children already are sampling the future via electronic rulers, electronic spellers, and even electronic building blocks.

Thus, if educators believe that the world is in a period of rapid growth and accelerated change, if educators believe the future does not merely represent 1984 or 1994, or 2004, but rather, right now, this minute, and if educators believe the purpose of education is to reflect and perpetuate society as well as help create a new society, then the critical issue that education must address itself to is assuming not how far it has come or where it is today, but what it needs to do to help youth cope with a new world yet to be discovered. But education cannot be satisfied with just helping youth cope. If education is to give youth the skills to help create their own future, it must address itself to how education can help youth thrive and excel.

Two options are available to education in dealing with this situation. Quite simply stated, education can either accept or reject the premise that the world will, indeed, be significantly different. In reality, however, there is really only one choice. Thus, adopting the premise that the world will be different seems to be the only way to fly because ignoring it could result in even greater catastrophe, namely, educational obsolescence.

Environmentalists generally concur that within the next 20 years 500,000 species of plant and animal life will become extinct. Also in danger of becoming extinct is public education. Why? Not because of loss of local control although that would be a popular response, but because there is serious doubt as to whether it is effectively fulfilling the major functions for which it was intended -- to reflect as well as perpetuate the American society.

Schools today can be likened to a time machine because students passing through school doors take a step back into history. What better place to find remnants of the 50's - namely books, bells, and yes, even back to basics. Unfortunately, schools bear little resemblance to today's post-industrialized, computerized, and transformized world as described in the writings of Bell (The Coming of Post-Industrial Society), Harman (An Incomplete Guide to the Future), Toffler (Future Shock, The Third Wave), Theobald (Beyond Despair: Directions for America's Third Century), Kahn (The Year 2000, The Next Two Hundred Years), and the Club of Rome (No Limits to Learning: Bridging the Human Gap). Ironically, in addition to describing the crises of crisis nature of the world, these futurists also describe a world which is in the process of being caught up in a spirit of new discovery to confront these crises - a spirit characterized by imaginativeness, creativity, innovation, and experimentation. It is a spirit that is vehement, vibrant, and bold. It is a spirit that can be likened to the pilgrims on the Mayflower who were on the threshold of discovering a new world. This is the spirit of new discovery that is prerequisite to meet the challenges of a changing, complex, and confusing world. Unmistakenly, it is an exciting time to be alive. It is exciting because all can have a stake in the operation, all can help make decisions to create a new world, and all can be Apollos. The new frontier is not outer space, it is here - planet earth.

Believing that schools are doing an adequate job of perpetuating the American society, deserves a "D" for making a "dangerous" assumption concerning the state of the art of public schools. Much evidence exists to show that schools are remiss in this vital function. The dissatisfaction of the public stemming from their lack of confidence in schools is but one example. Another example is indicated by Robert Samples' research (The Metaphoric Mind) on the hemispheres of the brain. He points out that schools have overemphasized left hemisphere learning (sequential, linear, logical) at the expense of the right hemisphere development. This becomes all the more critical when one realizes that it is the right hemisphere which is called upon to find solutions to current problems which involve intuitive, creative, imaginative type reasoning. However, this is nit-picking compared to the discrepancy one finds after an examination of where society is at and headed when compared to where schools are at and where they are headed. For example, whereas society is pluralistic, schools are monolithic, whereas society is integrated, schools are fragmented, and whereas society is changing, moving forward, schools are holding fast to seven period days and stepping backwards.

PART II

Stimulating Encounters Of An Unendangered
Kind: A Futurist-Educator

What can schools do to remove themselves from the endangered species list? First, all educators need to focus on two futuristic process goals.   These processes involve (1) helping youth cope with tomorrow today because, indeed, that is education's biggest challenge and (2) helping to make the future more real for students because, indeed, that is where they will be spending the rest of their lives. The former involves the need to develop a new list of surviving/thriving skills and the latter deals with the area of future studies which should be integrated into all curricula.

To better understand futuristics as applied to education, the writings and speeches of Glines (Educational-Futures, I, II, III, IV), Pino ("The Future is Now"), Shane (Curriculum for the 21st Century), and Barnes (1996: A Look Back at Educational Transitions) should be required reading and listening for all public school educators. A review of these writings will indicate that futuristics does not mean teachers have to subscribe to Science Fiction Quarterly; futuristics does not mean administrators have to purchase a crystal ball; and futuristics does not mean school boards have to build miniature "space mountains." Of most importance, futuristics does not mean having to scratch everything and reinvent the wheel. Futuristics does, however, mean education may have to discard some worn, used spokes, as well as add some completely new ones in the form of philosophies, programs, and practices having a future focus emphasizing less what was good in the past for students, but more of what will be good in the future for students.

A second step would be to sort out the relevant from the irrelevant in terms of curriculum priorities which help youth cope with tomorrow today and which help make the future more real for youth. Because the best teaching ever is occurring in today's schools, there are things being done which are relevant and have a futuristic focus. For example, the concern for developing self-esteem is refreshing and certainly a need of everyone as we face a world characterized by little permanence and much change. Unfortunately, even this concern has taken a backseat as education takes a step backwards to the basics. Thus, the notion of what should be our educational priorities is a fundamental one which can only be determined after a look into the future.

The third step for public education is in the form of a challenge. The challenge is to instill a spirit of new discovery into the hearts and minds of every educator in America's public schools. The spirit of new discovery necessitates education having some heroes, some new pioneers, some schools and people to model who are willing to take a risk and begin putting into practice what futurists and futurist-educators are saying.

The spirit of new discovery involves re-educating the public in order to help them to understand the "new basics." The basic skills such as cooperating, valuing, discovering, choosing, creating and communicating need to be wrapped by warm, caring teachers in an attractive box labeled the "real basics." At a time when basics are analogous to gasoline at 21 cents a gallon, anything labeled basics has an excellent chance of being bought, especially when these new basics are fundamental to survival.

The spirit of new discovery involves becoming a futurist-educator. What is a futurist-educator?

First and foremost, a futurist-educator is a caring/sensitive human being. They literally adopt their students during the time they are in their classroom. The notion of teaching children as if they were your own is very valid. With the deterioration of the family unit, the need for counseling of today's youth has never been greater. Without a caring, sensitive attitude coupled with high expectations for students, little of worth can be accomplished.

A futurist-educator is a positive thinker. Proactive teachers are those which discriminate between the essential and the non-essential. Proactive teachers plan curricula first in terms of its meaningfulness in meeting current and future needs of kids rather than planning curricula on the basis of it having met some need in the past. This means selecting curriculum which aids the student in helping him/her better understand the future. When today's 5 year olds will be spending two thirds of their lives in the 21st century, focusing curriculum on the world they will be living in seems to make a lot of sense. For example, students find history more interesting when past, present, and future are given equal time. In times of rapid change, teachers need to do a better job of anticipating events prior to their occurring. The best model to follow here is the flight guide. In other words, we don't start from the present (where we are), we start from the future (where we want to go) and plan on how to get there.

A futurist-educator is a risk taker. There is no room for complacency, stagnation, or mediocrity in today's education. Focusing educational goals on the future involves doing something different which involves taking a risk. Nothing of significance has ever occured without the element of risk. At a time when education has reverted back to the dark ages, more devil's advocates, more vice presidents for heresy, more revolutionaries need to characterize our teaching profession. Education has had its "time out."

A futurist-educator places an increased emphasis on process and the adoption of the idea that process equals content. With an exponential growth of knowledge, discovering how to find information or learning how to learn becomes all important. The importance of knowing which states border Kansas may be questionable. Knowing how to find the answer when needed is a must.

In the final analysis, the spirit of new discovery for public school educators means meeting the challenge and the commitment to adequately prepare today's students to be ready for the future. As today's students ready themselves to pioneer the third century, skills enabling them to create their own future will be required. Indeed, what is more important?

PART III

Rewarding Encounters Of A Creating Kind: A Futurized Curriculum

A primary goal of every teacher should be to not merely meet the needs of their students, but more importantly, to help them realize and discover new needs. Although this is a primary intent of this publication, it should not be mistaken to be a resource solely for helping teachers help students. Rather, this publication is also intended to help teachers help themselves. How?

At a time in which the only major movement in education is the movement of teachers out of the profession, teachers need to discover ways in which they feel they are making a difference in the lives of students; they need to discover ways enabling themselves to not merely survive but thrive. This can be accomplished by developing those attitudes and actions which result in having a stake in the future lives of their students. Unfortunately, too many teachers believe that whatever they do really does not make that much difference due to all of the other variables (e.g., television) that enter a student's growth. Other teachers feel the added pressures and responsibilities are not worth the risk of an ulcer and an overdraft, not to mention a physical confrontation with students.

The notion that teaching today is not what it used to be is very real to teachers. Consequently, this dissolution, dissatisfaction, and distress is causing many to search for the real meaning of their teaching self. The answer to this question lies not in the past but in the future. It is the future teachers need to help students discover and by doing so, they will re-discover themselves. Why? Because they will begin to understand why they, more than anyone else, have the most critical role to play in pioneering students to cope with tomorrow today.

Vis a vis the changing family unit, teachers have been given a "carte blanche" to help students meet the demands of an ever increasingly complex, confused, and changing society. Teachers have a captive audience and a green light to proceed to not just perpetuate society but, if need be, to help change society.

The idea of preparing youth for the future is not new to education. Any school philosophy undoubtedly, will mention that a fundamental purpose of schooling is to prepare kids for life. Educators who write such philosophies have good intentions but with the increasing number of staffings, student disruptions, and teacher evaluations, re-assessing the worth of present programs in terms of meeting future needs as described in the philosophy is seldom undertaken. If it is done, the discrepancy model generally used is a regional accrediting association which emphasizes programs based on what was good in the past rather than programs having a future focus. Whereas schools do have the future focused philosophy, now they need to match it with programs and practices.

There are a number of ways to incorporate futuristics into a school program. A common practice is via a course in future studies. The work of Kauffman (Teaching the Future) is an excellent guide for implementing such a course. Another alternative is to teach a unit in future studies. LaConte's publication Teaching Tomorrow Today is a good source to obtain practical information on what to include in such a futures unit. Although there are other approaches that could be explored, the futuristic process approach for which this publication is intended involves integrating futuristics into what is currently being taught. In many respects, it involves teaching the "old stuff" with a new purpose, namely to help students cope with tomorrow today via futuristic processes and to help make the future more real for students via future studies activities.

Adopting such an approach will accomplish a number of things. First, it will not isolate the study of the future, but rather, help students begin to understand the relevancy of today's curriculum because it will be dealing with content that they find important and meaningful namely, the future.

Second, it will allow teachers to teach the basics but with a new twist, a new reason, while at the same time accomplishing the primary goals of schools.

Third, studying the future has a built in motivation factor for students because they find such learning to be exciting, stimulating, and, above all, relevant. Why not? They are learning about the world in which they will be living.

Fourth, as students begin growing in the futuristic processes (to be discussed later) and as students begin showing a greater awareness of the world around them and the world of tomorrow, teachers will begin feeling that they do have a stake in the operation and that they can and are making a difference in the lives of their students.

Fifth, undertaking this approach will necessitate no additional facilities, faculty, or finances. In addition, little, if any, extra time is needed to incorporate such studies into the curriculum because teachers can continue to do what they are currently doing. The changes that are required are in the attitudes of teachers as they begin becoming concerned about their students' futures growth.

Implementation of the activities contained in this book will futurize a classroom in two important ways. First, all of the activities emphasize a futuristic process which is intended to help students cope with tomorrow today. Second, the majority of the activities deal with some future studies activity which is intended to help make the future more real for students.

The futuristic processes serving as a target for all of the activities are (1) creating, (2) valuing, (3) choosing, (4) communicating, (5) cooperating, (6) discovering. They are defined and illustrated in the following outline.

Process Skills Needed To Help Youth
Create Tomorrow - Today

COPING, SURVIVING, THRIVING

CREATING   VALUING   CHOOSING
COMMUNICATING   COOPERATING   DISCOVERING

CREATING: those activities which provide students the opportunity to become involved in improving some aspect of society existing now or in the future, making something new for the betterment of society, or improving their creating, imagining potential.

VALUING: those activities which provide students the opportunity to become involved in examining their beliefs to better understand themselves and others and to facilitate decision-making.

CHOOSING: those activities which provide students the opportunity to become involved in a decision making process involving choosing from a number of alternatives.

COMMUNICATING: those activities which provide students the opportunity to become involved in expressing one's ideas, opinions, and feelings to others in a positive manner as well as being able to communicate (i.e., relate) with oneself.

COOPERATING: those activities which provide students the opportunity to become involved in working with others.

DISCOVERING: those activities which provide students the opportunity to become involved in using existing knowledge to discover other knowledge.

GIVENS: the present school curriculum.

Why These Six Process Areas?

A Meeting Of Super Teacher Teachers

No great amount of research has been undertaken to support the inclusion of these six process areas into curricula.   On the other hand, because applied research has usually led to a common sense conclusion, common sense has been employed in selecting them.   The logic used in their selection can be better understood by the following narrative.

Super teacher teachers have just arrived from outer space to solve our schooling problems regarding the determination of what is essential for schools to teach.   They know nothing about our society -- it's past, its present, or its future.   They have been invited to a meeting with a group of educational leaders for the sole purpose of answering this question, "What should schools teach to provide youth the essential skills necessary to function successfully in our society?" After hearing the question that pinpoints their assignment, the super teacher teachers huddle and after just a few minutes, they make this request.   "In order for us to accurately deal with this question, it is important for us to know what your society is like now, what it has been like, and what you believe it will be like?"   After hearing a lengthy discussion by the educational leaders concerning the past and present of society and some speculative, uncertain notions about its future, the super teacher teachers again huddle and after a few minutes, with the educational leaders anxiously awaiting their conclusion, issue this statement.   "It appears as if your society has undergone a great deal of change during its 200 year history.   The changes having the greatest impact on society have come about within the past 25-40 years.   Although you do not have a definite answer on what the future holds for you, all indications point to your future society being different from your present society which implies that major changes will continue to occur. And, what these major changes will be, no one knows for sure. Undoubtedly, some will be a negative force on your society and some a positive force. The essential skills required of your students should reflect a changing world."

Upon hearing this statement, the educational leaders began to make bewildered and somewhat frustrating glances at one another. A disappointed hush fell over the audience. Quickly analyzing the reactions of the leaders, the super teachers also began to appear nervous and somewhat perplexed. Their spokesperson asked, "Can we be of further help to you?"

The spokesperson for the leaders quietly stood and with a look of dismay said, "I believe I speak for my colleagues when I say I am disappointed with your statement. We expected to find some answers, you merely told us what we already know."

A murmur of amazement quickly engulfed the super teacher teachers. Almost in complete unison they burst forth, "You mean you were already aware of this?"

"Why certainly," said the educational leaders. "What you said is no revelation to us."

"Then why have you requested that we help you in deciding what you should teach your youth? You possess all the information you need to make such a decision," the super teacher spokesperson said, becoming annoyed. "What your curriculum should consist of in order for your youth to function successfully in society is the integration of skills which transcend any barriers or obsolescence created by change."

After huddling briefly with the other super teacher teachers, their spokesperson continued, "It is our recommendation in view of the fact that you have apparently not acted upon what is happening in society that you immediately integrate the following process areas in your school program to more accurately reflect the society around you, and, more importantly, to provide your youth the skills to successfully and effectively deal with changes in their society and lives. In addition, because no time can be wasted, we recommend that you incorporate these skills into what you are already doing."

The processes recommended for integration into the present curriculum to enable youth to successfully live in society are the following:

Discovering

The mushrooming of knowledge calls for people to become less skilled in regurgitating information and more skilled in the process of discovering how to find information when needed. Becoming familiar with the use of (a) human and non-human resources, (b) forecasting techniques, (c) problem solving, and (d) becoming a wise consumer and producer should enable people to cope with an information over-load.

Creating

It is easy for youth today to become negative about the future with television giving greater percentages of time to bad news, not to mention the number of critical concerns facing the world. Also, people in general, talk about when they lived in the "good old days" which implies that good days will never return. Youth need to feel they can do something to create a better world for themselves and society. Participating in activities which are intended to improve their imagining and creating potentials will help them generate ideas to build a better world. In addition, this process involves giving greater time to the pluses in society and less to the minuses.

Choosing

Being able to make effective decisions is becoming increasingly important especially when they are frequently being called to be made overnight and when one realizes that decisions made today shape tomorrow. Being able to make decisions about using time wisely, about the pros and cons of using drugs, alcohol, and other "tripping" alternatives, about choosing a career, about family planning involve the process of choosing from a set of alternatives. The whole notion of "alternative futures" implies a choice among varying types of futures. Correct decisions made today will determine the quality of such a future.

Communicating

Being able to understand oneself is of vital importance in a complex and confused world. The growing emphasis on self-help and personal growth books and seminars is an indication that people are searching for a better understanding of themselves and where they fit in today's society. The importance of developing self-esteem in students today is an indication that schools have given attention to this process. The move from an independent society to an interdependent society necessitates people being able to express their ideas to others as well as to empathize with others. A trend for an increase in human relations experiences for teachers is on target. However, more emphasis on the same skills for students is also needed. One indication that human relations processes need to be pushed with more vigor is the decline in number of students taking foreign languages in the United States.

Cooperating

Becoming more interdependent means becoming aware of the fact that decisions we make as individuals or countries impact on others which necessitates skills in working with people. Closely related to communicating, the process of cooperating involves growth in how to function effectively in a group. Our society does an excellent job of building in a spirit of competition. Changes in our world necessitates giving cooperation equal time. Activities involving cooperation involve having students record the number of times they help someone in a week or working with someone on a project that they might not normally work with.

Valuing

Why has the trend toward incorporating values clarification exercises in schools been so popular in recent years? No doubt people have been searching for answers to deal with racism, sex stereotyping, abortion, genetic manipulation, and other issues that confront people today. No longer do individuals have a ready answer for what is "the good life." Parents are permitting their children to make many decisions themselves because they are gradually becoming more accepting of alternative patterns of living. The process of valuing is especially important in a futuristic curriculum because answers to current crises depend on the values we possess. However, it isn't just a matter of clarifying values, but rather, what action will be taken to demonstrate such values. For example, it may be fine for students to believe that their schools should look nice, but are they willing to actively participate in a school grounds beautification plan?

Integration Of Futuristic Processes

Where does the present school curriculum fit in? It has a very special function in that it serves as the vehicle by which the processes are delivered. Activity Number 1, "Alien Encounter," for example, could be used as an introduction to a lesson review in punctuation or sentence structure in the area of language arts. It could also be used as a culminating activity, giving the students something to which they can look forward or even as a positive reinforcer for doing their work. The activity could also be utilized as the main activity in a lesson or even a test exercise.

Activity number 38, "Tomorrow's Oscars," could be integrated into a social studies lesson focusing on entertainment. Using the activity as an "attention getter", main attraction, part of a unit, or culminating activity is bound to stimulate more interest in the students as well as enthusiasm in the teacher because of its uniqueness.

The six futuristic process skills emphasized in the activities are really the hidden agenda for each activity. Through participation in the activities, K-12 students are also becoming skillful in areas currently having "back seat status" in school or are avoided altogether. The processes are emphasized as equally as important as the content to be learned and, in reality, are the content.

In addition to futurizing the present curriculum, they also serve as threads which tie the total curriculum together. While teachers may be teaching their own thing in language arts, social studies, or math, if their activities reflect the six futuristic processes, the total will have the necessary ingredients enabling students to cope with tomorrow today.

In summary, implementation of the activities is not difficult because they are designed to parallel what is currently being taught. Thus, they can be used in an introduction to a lesson or attention getting strategy, as a closing activity to leave the students with a "hey, let's do it again attitude," or they can be used as the main attraction of any given lesson to give the students something to look forward to.

Whatever one does in the area of futuristics, there are some important factors that need to be considered.

Some Do's About Futurizing

1) Do consider seriously what is being done to make the future real for your students. Do you know if your students have a positive or negative attitude about the future? Remembering that the future is where youth will live, addressing these questions and more are guaranteed to excite and motivate students.

2) Do ask yourself what you are doing to help kids cope with tomorrow today. Do you emphasize the futuristic process skills mentioned earlier or does your teaching result in left brain learning? Generally, schools build for a climate of academically talented rather than creativity talented. This will need to change if youth are to gain the skills necessary to create their own future.

3) The trends toward more youth suicides, drugs, and "tripping" alternatives indicate a rather confused and insecure youth. It is of vital importance that youth develop a confident attitude concerning their ability to create a positive future not only for themselves but society as well. Do implement activities which permit students to achieve this goal.

4) It is easy for students to become negative about the future due to the many unresolved problems which impact on our lives today. These thunderstorms should take a back seat to the rainbows which emphasize the many good things that have taken place and which also reinforce the idea in number 3. Thus, do emphasize more rainbows than thunderstorms with the goal of having the students develop a positive attitude about the future.

5) Do allow students to see themselves in the future. Talking about the future will be of little worth unless the students can see how future possibilities and probabilities will affect their own lives. For example, if you have them write a 1996 headline, ask them how this happening will affect them.

6) Do follow through with the purpose of this publication and integrate futures activities into what you are currently doing rather than creating a separate course.

At a time when teachers are bombarded with more responsibilities, more pressures and more reasons to leave the profession, the futuristic process approach promises to be a refreshing retreat forward.

PART IV

Practical Encounters Of A Helping Kind: How To Use This Book

You will find in Part V "Teacher Action Pages" as well as "Student Activity Pages" that describe in detail forty-five activities that teachers can use to futurize their classroom. The "Teacher Action Pages" each contain four sections:

1) <u>count down</u> - refers to the title of the activity.

2) <u>focus</u> - refers to the purpose of the activity.

3) <u>target</u> - refers to the futuristic process to be emphasized.

4) <u>blast off</u> - refers to the description of the activity and methods of implementation. In some cases, there are also variations of the activity given.

No specific grade level has been given for the activities found on the "Student Activity Pages." A quick review, however, will indicate which activities are more aligned with children of the primary age as opposed to intermediate or upper elementary. All of the activities are intended to be integrated into the basic disciplines thereby fulfilling a primary purpose of this book, "to teach old stuff a new way." These activities are to be used also for teaching units in the six futuristic process areas.

Part VI contains a hundred starter ideas to initiate the development of other activities. A goodly number of futuristic bulletin board items will be found here.

FUTURISTIC PROCESS ACTIVITIES | BASIC DISCIPLINE ACTIVITIES

Activity No.	Choosing	Communicating	Co-operating	Creating	Discovering	Valuing		Language Arts	Social Studies	Math	Science
1		X		X				X			
2				X					X		X
3		X				X		X			
4				X	X						X
5				X							X
6				X				X	X	X	X
7		X			X			X	X		
8	X			X					X	X	X
9		X						X			
10					X						X
11				X					X		
12		X						X			
13				X					X		
14					X				X	X	X
15		X	X			X			X		
16				X				X			
17	X								X	X	X
18		X						X			
19		X	X		X				X		X
20				X					X		X
21			X			X			X		
22			X						X		
23		X						X	X	X	X
24	X								X		
25	X									X	
26				X				X			X
27	X								X	X	X
28		X							X		
29		X	X						X	X	
30					X			X	X	X	X
31					X				X		
32				X					X		
33					X			X			
34	X										X
35			X					X			
36			X			X					X
37	X			X					X		
38		X	X						X		
39	X					X			X		
40	X					X			X		
41		X									X
42		X				X					X
43				X						X	
44				X				X	X		X
45	X								X		

PART V

Exciting Encounters Of A How To Kind:
45 Futuristic Student Activities

This part provides an in-depth description of projects to be implemented in the classroom. They all evolved from an idea. Because few proven and practical futuristic classroom activities are available, teachers are encouraged to go further and develop a do-it-yourself attitude with regards to developing their own materials.

COUNT DOWN: Alien Encounter   **#1**

FOCUS: To provide students the opportunity to discuss the possibility of
                extraterrestial life and imagine what "they" would say to earth's
                people during the first alien encounter.

TARGET: Communicating, Creating

BLAST OFF: No direct evidence exists as to the reality of extraterrestial life,
                however, space probes have been landed on Mars and Venus and water
                has been found on both. Scientists have listening devices trained on
                the skies to encounter the first alien noises in the event that highly
                technological societies do exist. The exchange of information could
                be extremely beneficial. For example, they might have an answer to
                the energy problem, they may have ideas on how we can get along
                better with one another, or how to eliminate hunger. Have the
                students imagine that your classroom has a large radio-telescope
                aimed at outer space. One day, the class is interrupted by the sounds
                of the computer which is hooked up to the telescope. A student
                dashes over to the computer, tears off the print out, and reads it to
                the rest of the class. "Hello, I am an extraterrestial alien. I have
                a message for you. I have some questions and I have some answers."

                Using the student activity page, have the students write messages
                they believe this alien would say as well as develop some questions
                and some answers to solve current problems. Once completed, have
                individuals come to the front of the class to ask a question they
                wrote to the remainder of the class serving as aliens as well as
                reading their messages and giving some answers to world problems.

1
ALIEN ENCOUNTER

"Hello, I am an extraterrestial alien. I have a message for you. I have some questions and I have some answers."

Tell Me What You See

My Message:

_____

_____

_____

_____

My Questions:

_____

_____

_____

_____

My Answers:

_____

_____

_____

_____

THE INFORMATION YOU ASKED FOR FROM ?

FOCUS: To provide students the opportunity to solve the energy problem.

TARGET: Creating

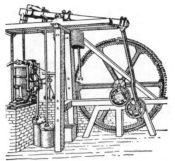

WATT'S STEAM-ENGINE

BLAST OFF: Begin by telling the students that a 10 year old student has just discovered the solution to the energy problem. It is something that no one would ever dream of using and it is something that we see and use every day. On the student activity page, have students draw a picture of this discovery. Emphasize that it is not one of the more common energy alternatives (i.e., coal, sun, wind, etc.), but could be such things as bubble gum, snow, pencils, etc. Having drawn the pictures, call on the students to show their discovery. Ask questions commonly asked about energy solutions: Is it expensive? How would you convert it for fuel? Is it available in large quantities? Will the supply ever run out? What would be a major disadvantage? What would be an advantage?

Variation: Have students give their own commercials to sell the discovery.

TINDER BOX, FLINT, AND STEEL.

HOWE'S SEWING
MACHINE

DISCOVERY!

I found the answer to the energy problem. Here is a picture of my discovery. It is something we see and use every day.

**THE ENERGY WAR:
BREW IT YOURSELF**

AN ENERGY SAVER

COUNT DOWN: Me Tree   **#3**

FOCUS: To provide students the opportunity to know themselves and the
                person they want to be.

TARGET: Valuing, Communicating

BLAST OFF: If change continues to characterize our way of life in the future, the
                ability to know ourselves will become increasingly important as we
                strive to cope with a changing, complex, confusing, and challenging
                society.   Begin by identifying with the students as many words or
                phrases which describe themselves (i.e., tall, like to play piano,
                friendly, active, nervous, talkative, etc.). About 50% of the words
                should be personality traits and the remainder things which the
                student likes to do. Put these items on chalkboard or on a ditto.
                Using the student activity page, have each student write in the words
                or phrases which describe him/her "now" on the "now" side of the me
                tree. On the "future" side of the tree, have the students write in the
                words or phrases which they would like to be descriptive of
                themselves in the future. Once completed, they could be shared in
                circle discussion sessions, kept personal, or to use in student/teacher
                conferences.

                Variation: (1) use words which describe personalities as a vocabulary
                review or spelling words.   (2) using large butcher paper, cut out
                pictures of things which describe them and put them on a "me tree."

32

<u>MY ME TREE</u>

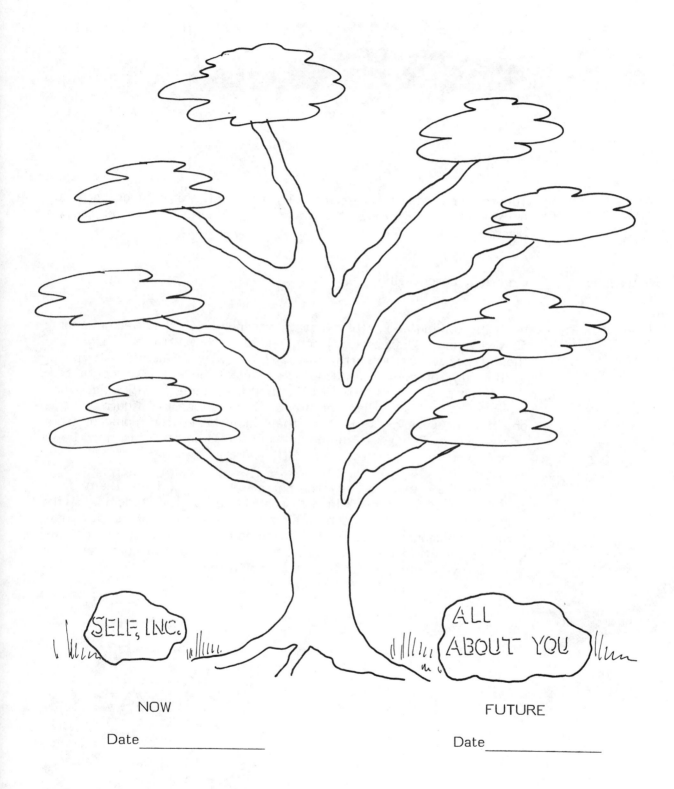

SELF, INC.

ALL
ABOUT YOU

NOW

FUTURE

Date_____

Date_____

FOCUS: To provide students the opportunity to create future transportation models and consider how this would be an improvement over today's transportation.

TARGET: Creating, Discovering

BLAST OFF: Begin by talking about the types of transportation that were available 50 years ago. Discuss land, sea, and air transportation. Compare those types with transportation existing now in terms of cost, speed, availability, problems resulting, etc. Next have the students talk about the types of transportation that they believe will exist when they are 21. Have them create a three dimension figure of this object using various "stuff" that they could bring from home or from things you may have available in your classroom. This may be a project you may wish to team with your art teacher.

Prior to their making the transportation models, have them draw three types of air, sea, or land transportation on the student activity page. From these three, they are to select one to construct for their three dimensional model. When completed, allow time for the students to introduce their models to the class and discuss why they are improvements over today's transportation.

4
GETTING AROUND WHEN I'M 21

I am now_____years old.

The year is_____. In the year_____I will be 21.

_____

When I'm 21 this is what I will use to get around in the air.

FLYING SAUCERS

_____

When I'm 21 this is what I will use to get around in the water.

_____

When I'm 21 this is what I will use to get around on land.

The young must try their wings.

FOCUS: To provide students the opportunity to speculate on what exists on unexplored planets.

TARGET: Creating

BLAST OFF: All of us have an idea on what may or may not exist on planets that are yet to be explored. This is also a favorite imagining activity for students as well. Also, by speculating on the type of life or non-life on other planets provides a launching pad for further study of extraterrestial life. Imagine with the students that you just landed on one of the unknown planets and, behold, you have encountered some strange creatures. They appear to be one half plant and one half animal. Some that you can recognize immediately are carrotaffe (carrot-giraffe), rosig (rose-pig), potape (potato-ape). Have the students draw and label their plant-ams on the student activity page. Also talk about what plant and animal life may exist on some of the better known planets.

CREATURES
OF THE
THIRD PLANET

It's name is _____

COUNT DOWN: What if . . . . .   **# 6**

FOCUS: To provide students the opportunity to stimulate right hemisphere of
                brain by speculating on some "What if" type questions.

TARGET: Creating

BLAST OFF: A simple but effective strategy for stimulating the right hemisphere
                learning in children is to pose "What if" questions to them. Below are
                a number of questions to ask your students. Place these on the
                chalkboard. On the student activity page are four squares. In each
                square, the students are to draw their response to 4 of your "What
                if" questions. Having completed the 4 drawings, have the students
                share their papers with their neighbors. Can they guess what the
                person's response would be as shown in the drawings? At the bottom
                of the page, the students are to generate their own "What if"
                questions.

1.   What if you discovered a solution to the energy crisis, what
      would it be?

2.   What if you had a billion dollars, what would you do to spend
      it in one day?

3.   What if you could invent one invention that you know would
      work, what would it be?

4.   What if you could see yourself 25 years from now, what would
      you see?

5.   What if you were the world's strongest person, what would you
      do?

6.   What if you could change the way people feel, how would you
      change them?

7.   What if you could do anything you wanted to do today in school,
      what would it be?

8.   If you could have 100 of one thing, what would it be?

Variation: The questions used in this activity could be specifically
drafted at almost any content area thereby allowing easy integration.

6

DIRECTIONS: Write a "What if" question in each box. Answer the question with a drawing. At the bottom of the page write your own "What if" question.

What if_____
_____
_____
_____

What if_____
_____
_____
_____

What if_____
_____
_____
_____

What if_____
_____
_____
_____

My "What if" question:_____
_____
_____
_____

WHAT IF ?

COUNT DOWN: Headlines: 2011   #7

FOCUS: To provide students the opportunity to conceptualize future events and their own lives in the future.

TARGET: Discovering, Communicating

BLAST OFF: An interesting activity for helping to make the future more real for students is to imagine it is 2011 and they just picked up the Society Times morning newspaper (assuming there is one). What might the headlines read? Space is provided on the student activity page for students to write their headline. Discuss with them the likelihood of this headline actually occurring and what caused them to write this headline. Are there trends today which would lead one to believe that this might actually occur? Is the headline an optimistic or pessimistic view of the future? In the next portion of the activity page, the students are to write a My Times headline about themselves in the year 2011. Discussion of this headline should involve asking students if the headline written previously would have any impact on their personal headline. What is the likelihood of their personal headline occurring? What things would need to take place to bring this about? Is it pessimistic or optimistic?

SOCIETY TIMES   MY TIMES

PEACE PILLS
FOR
LEADERS?

The year is 2011. Write a headline for the <u>Society Times</u> newspaper.

The year is 2011. Write a headline about something important that happened to you this year for the <u>My Times</u> newspaper.

 # 8

FOCUS: To provide students the opportunity to design a better world and to decide what things constitute an A+ world.

TARGET: Creating, Choosing

BLAST OFF: Many improvements can be made to improve our world. Students have an amazing sense of direction when thinking of ideas for these improvements. Begin by talking about the strengths and weaknesses of today's world. A good technique for doing this is to tear apart a newspaper -- giving each article a grade depending upon whether it describes a positive or a negative happening in our society (i.e., "A's" for most positive, "F's" for most negative). Pose the questions to the group - what changes would you make in order that the "A's" and "B's" out weigh the "D's" and "F's" or what changes would you make to bring about an A+ world? Use the student activity form to help in this process.

Variation: In completing items 5 and 6 on the student activity page, ask students to think about how their changes do or do not involve any scientific or mathematical concepts. Invariably, in order for changes to come about, math and science would need to be involved (e.g., designing a temperature controlled city for 50,000 people).

8
MY A+ WORLD

1. It is called _____

2. Its symbol is_____

3. Three important laws are:

    _____

    _____

    _____

    _____

4. Two characteristics of its people are:

    _____

    _____

    _____

    _____

5. Two things which make my world better than the world where
    I currently live are:

    _____

    _____

    _____

6. The first step that the current world needs to do to become
    an A+ world is:

    _____

    _____

    _____

The Most Important Spelling List   **#9**

FOCUS: In order for people to cope with tomorrow's world, they will need a strong feeling of identity. This activity is designed to help fulfill this need.

TARGET: Communicating

K I N G

BLAST OFF: Some of the first words that the children should learn to spell at the beginning of the year are their classmates' first and last names. Proceed the way you normally would in your spelling program, but emphasize that "this is the way John's name is spelled and this is the way Sally's name is spelled, etc." After giving a quiz on the names, have the student who owns that name spell it for the students. Don't forget to add your name. The next list could be principals, other teachers, custodians, cooks, etc.

LEADER

President

MONARCH

PRIME MINISTER

9
THE MOST IMPORTANT SPELLING LIST

Can you spell them correctly?   Use the guide to study from.

NAMES OF STUDENTS IN CLASS

First Name	Last Name
1.	
2.	
3.	
4.	
5.	
6.	
7.	
8.	
9.	
10.	
11.	
12.	
13.	
14.	
15.	
16.	
17.	
18.	
19.	
20.	
21.	
22.	
23.	
24.	
25.	

Teacher's name

FOCUS: To provide students the opportunity to assess the pros and cons of technological advances.

TARGET: Discovering

BLAST OFF: One of the greatest advances in technology has been the automobile. However, recently people have been forgetting many of the pluses and have raised a good many questions about its minuses. With the students, list (identify) some pros and cons regarding the auto. Next have each student select a technological advancement and have him/her go through the same exercise. Allow the students to present their particular technology to the class giving the pros and cons. With all the students in the class, brainstorm a solution for one of the shortcomings.

10
THE AUTOMOBILE: GOOD OR BAD

What's your opinion about the automobile? List what you believe to be its strengths and weaknesses.

The Automobile:
_____

Strengths	Weaknesses
1.	1.
2.	2.
3.	3.
4.	4.
5.	5.

_____

Identify another invention that has seemingly made life better. Identify the strengths and weaknesses of this invention. In addition, select one weakness and provide one possible solution.

Technological Advancement
_____

Strengths	Weaknesses
1.	1.
2.	2.
3.	3.
4.	4.
5.	5.

_____

A solution for weakness No._____would be: (Explain)

AUTO-RACING WARS

HOW MUCH SHOULD YOU PAY FOR GAS?

FOCUS: To provide students the opportunity to experience success in learning about the future and, subsequently, to help them develop a positive attitude towards it.

TARGET: Creating

BLAST OFF: Positive attitudes about the future are not automatic. Also, finding success in studying the future is not automatic. However, both the positive attitude and the success are important. The completion statements on the student activity page are intended to help kids deal with the future, but more importantly, to help them find success because there is no "wrong" answer. As a result, students should begin to feel good about discussing the future because they can find success. After allowing kids time to complete the statements, go over them as a class. Call on those students who are in need of finding success in school.

Variation: This would be an excellent activity to place in a future learning center.

11
Fill In Your Future

Answer the questions by filling in the blank space.

1. In what year will you become a grandparent?_____

2. What will you do on the first day of your retirement?

    _____

3. What will be the title of the best movie of the year in 2001?

    _____

4. What's the first question you will ask your home computer?

    _____

5. A modern house of 2011 will look something like:_____

    _____

    _____

6. The most famous artifact found by archeologists in the year
    2500 will be_____

7. Three new words originated in the year 1988 are_____,

    _____, and_____.

8. The most popular toy parents will buy children twelve years from
    now will be_____

9. When your children are five years old, their favorite TV program
    will be_____

10. My favorite hobby in the year 1993 will be_____

11. My greatest fear for the future is_____

    _____

12. Your parents are looking foward to their future because

    _____

    _____

MORE THAN JUST
ONE STEP BEYOND

FOCUS: To help students realize their strengths, understand and get to know one another, realize how others perceive them, and to help students discover strengths they wish to develop in themselves for the future.

TARGET: Communicating

BLAST OFF: (a) Discuss with students the notion that all of us have strengths and that all of us have positive things we can say about ourselves. Some of these things are physical things or things you do well (i.e., being a good ice skater, dancer, read, etc.) Some are things which describe the way we act (e.g., friendly, caring, leader, etc.) For younger students, list many of these things on the board.

(b) Using the activity page, students first sign their name at the bottom and then complete top third of the paper where they identify their strengths.

(c) With top third of paper folded under, collect and redistribute papers.

(d) Looking at name on paper, students write down at least 5 strengths they perceive about this person.

(e) Collect and hand papers back to owners.

(f) Owners compare strengths they wrote down about themselves and what their classmates perceived about them; undoubtedly, there will be some discrepancies.

(g) The last step is to have students write down some strengths they would like to work on in the future.

(h) Variation 1: After activity is completed, collect papers and read off the strengths listed on each paper. After each one, students guess and see which person belongs to that paper.
Variation 2: Students identify one thing they can do now to achieve a future strength.

MY STRENGTHS:
TODAY AND TOMORROW

Some of my strengths and good things about myself are:

(Fold here when finished)

The strengths or good things about this person whose name is at the bottom are:

_____

Some strengths and good things I would like to have are:

NAME_____

NOW EVEN BETTER!

FOCUS: To help youth realize the importance of living now by taking advantage of resources in their own community.

TARGET: Creating

BLAST OFF: A common shortcoming of futures studies is the danger of living too much in the future.   Youth need to be reminded that they have an obligation to themselves to get the most out of life by living more in the now. A frequent complaint of youth is that they have nothing to do. However, an analysis of free things to do in their community and surrounding area can provide many things of interest.   This can be facilitated by helping students identify all of the things that can be done without cost.   Divide the class into small groups (4-6) and distribute a student activity page to each student.   In their groups, the students are to identify items in their community that they could do in their spare time without cost. With the entire class, have each group identify their list of things to do. As they are being identified, compile the lists on butcher paper. While this is being done, students are to add any new items to their lists.   How many items did you identify? How many things were new to some students? How many things could be done at any time during the year? What things could be done after school? This weekend?

Variation: Prepare lists of free things to do to give to the entire student body. A list might also be given to the local newspaper.

Centering ON NOW.

Are you living in the past present or future? While it is important to study and remember the past and to study the future, it is equally important that we live in the now. In other words, you need to take advantage of every opportunity to live life to its fullest. There are many things you can do in your community and surrounding area without cost. What are some things you can do merely for the asking?

Free Things To Do In My Community

1. _____ 9. _____

2. _____ 10. _____

3. _____ 11. _____

4. _____ 12. _____

5. _____ 13. _____

6. _____ 14. _____

7. _____ 15. _____

8. _____ 16. _____

FREE FREE free FREE FREE

FOCUS: To provide students the opportunity to discover that there are many things occurring that are improving our lives.

TARGET: Discovering

BLAST OFF: It is easy for students to develop a negative attitude about the future realizing that news both on TV and in the papers capitalizes on the negative.   Why?   Because if there were more good news than bad news, it would not be news.   In any event, it is important that students face their future with optimism.   The student activity page provides the opportunity for students to write down what they know to be good things happening.   An example in the area of medicine could be the fact that small pox has been eradicated due to vaccine. Students may choose improvements that have happened locally or nationally.   You may wish to have students work in small groups. Also, use the information gathered by students to put in a scrapbook or devote a bulletin board to the good things happening.

Variation: Rather than do the assignment in class, have students do it as a homework assignment asking their parents to help them.   With each improvement listed, have students identify how math or science was or was not involved.

THE FUTURE: A BETTER PLACE TO LIVE

Many things are happening in your community and/or world that are making it a better place to live. Within each area listed below, identify one good thing that is happening.

AREA	SOMETHING GOOD
Transportation	_____
Schools	_____
Cities	_____
Recreation	_____
Senior Citizens	_____
Wild Life	_____
Buildings	_____
Energy	_____
Medicine	_____
Foods	_____

"You've Got to Be Optimistic"

THERE HAS NEVER BEEN A BETTER TIME

FOCUS: As we begin to move from an independent society to an inter-
                dependent society and from a hierarchical to an interacting society,
                people will need to be closer in touch with their feelings. This
                activity is designed to help kids identify their feelings and determine
                their worth to them.

TARGET: Cooperating, Communicating, Valuing

BLAST OFF: Begin by having students in large or small groups, brainstorm the
                various kinds of feelings (i.e., excited, sadness, joyful, depressed,
                enthusiastic, tired, compassion, powerful, etc.) Try to obtain a
                minimum of 25-30 words describing various feelings. Place these in
                column one on the student activity page. In column two, the students
                are to place one check by those they used in the past week, in column
                three a check for those used yesterday, in column 4 a check beside
                the three they value most. In column five, a check beside the three
                feelings they wish they could express more often.

                The next step is the auction. In column six, the students are to assign
                a monetary value (students are allotted $200 apiece) to the feelings
                they cherish most. Having assigned a monetary value to the feelings,
                the auction begins (the teacher serves as auctioneer). Column seven
                is used to record the feelings they were actually able to purchase.

                The follow-up discussion should focus on feelings which are most
                important to us, one's ability or inability to express these feelings, the
                feelings which we use most often, and what one can do to express
                more of our feelings.

15
FINDING AND AUCTIONING MY FEELINGS

In column 1, list as many different types of feelings as you can think of. In column 2, place a check beside those feelings you used this past week, in column 3, place a check beside those feelings you used yesterday, in column 4, a check beside the 3 feelings you valued most, and in column 5, a check beside the 3 feelings you wish you could use more often. For columns 6 and 7, wait for the teacher's directions.

1	2	3	4	5	6	7
Feelings	Past Week	Yester-day	Value Most	Wish To Use	$	Feelings Purchased

FOCUS:　　　　To provide students the opportunity to generate ideas contributing to the betterment of society.

TARGET:　　　Creating

A TRAVEL CLUB

BLAST OFF:　　Schools have their chess clubs, ski clubs, camera clubs, glee clubs, etc. Few clubs in school, however, are established for the sole purpose of improving society. Introduce the idea by discussing why clubs and organizations are formed. Identify types of clubs that exist in their school and community. Which clubs exist for the purpose of socializing, entertaining, providing a service, etc.? In thinking about the ways the school, the community, the nation could be improved, what kind of clubs might be formed to facilitate these needs? Individually or in small groups or with the class as a whole, use the student activity page to create a club which will improve tomorrow.

Variation: Use this as a special project in language arts. Designing slogans, posters, rules, etc. for a club requires exceptional clarity and direction in order to communicate concerns and purposes to others.

A NUMISMATIC CLUB

MY CLUB FOR TOMORROW

_____

!.   Club name_____

2.   Purpose of club_____

3.   Club slogan for bumper sticker or button is_____
     _____

4.   Three things this club will do

     A._____

     B._____

     C._____

5.   Three rules of the club are

     A._____

     B._____

     C._____

6.   Its members shall be_____
     _____

7.   The first thing it will do is_____
     _____

8.   A reason why our school, community, or country will be better
     because of this club is_____

     _____

     _____

_____

ENERGY:TOGETHERNESS

FOCUS: To help students become aware of increasing pressures on countries to make critical decisions affecting population growth.

TARGET: Choosing

BLAST OFF: NASA forecasts a world population of 7 billion in the year 2000. This is an increase of 3 billion in just 25 years. Countries already have growing pains causing catastrophic instances of starvation due to over-population. Leaders are having to make some cricital decisions to cope with this problem. The story on the student activity page illustrates one case in which a serious decision needs to be made regarding population. The students are first to read the story and either individually, small, or large groups, identify at least 3 alternative decisions open to the president of the country and second to select the decision they would make and why. This activity would serve as a good launching pad for other activities or units relating to population.

17
PEOPLE PROBLEMS

A young president of a small underdeveloped island nation is faced with a tough decision. He must decide whether or not to allow doctors to vaccinate the entire population against diseases that cause most of the deaths on the island.

At first, this seems like no problem at all and many would even call it a blessing. Other nearby islands vaccinated their population and it cut the death rate in half almost overnight. The result was that twice as many babies lived (for here is where cuts in death rate have the greatest effect). However, the per person food supply dropped sharply on the already near-starving islands.

The president realizes that better health can be spread widely in his country. However, there may be no increases in better schools and more jobs. In fact, employment may fall to a lower level than before. He knows also that starving people do not starve quietly, particularly those people who have "seen it better."

The president feels it is very possible that his young country will not be able to bear the population increase. But he also knows that, when given a choice between life or death, all people -- throughout history -- choose life over death. If his own people hear that he has decided to keep vaccination from their country, it could very well mean death for him.

Three things the president could do are:

1._____

2._____

3._____

If I were president, I would choose No._____

My reasons are:_____

_____

_____

_____

_____

An Impossible Dream?

FOCUS: The primary purpose of this activity is to help students think of themselves in the future. It can serve as a good introduction to forecasting.

TARGET: Communicating

BLAST OFF: To obtain a better feel for the future, students need to have the opportunity to project themselves into it. Tell the students that they are going to write a letter to themselves with a postmark dated 20 years from now. Have the students describe what they believe will be happening in their lives concerning their job, their home, their leisure time, etc. Addressing their writing to the questions on the student activity page may be helpful. Having completed the letter, discuss with the students possible and probable changes that are forecasted to occur about that time. Having discussed their forecasts, give students an opportunity to change their letters. Culminate the activity by having the students discuss their letters in small groups or each day have two or three students read their letters to the class or place them on the bulletin board. Culminate by having the students seal their letters and give them to someone with instructions to mail them 20 years from now. Naturally, this person would need to be someone who would know the whereabouts of the writer.

18
A LETTER TO MYSELF POSTMARKED 20 YEARS FROM TODAY

Directions: Imagine today's date is 20 years from now. Write a letter to yourself telling about your life at this time. You may wish to use the following questions to guide your writing.

1. Where will you be living?

2. Will you be married?

3. What will you be doing for recreation?

4. What will your job be like?

5. What kinds of things will you have in your home that you do not have now?

6. What kind of transportation will you have?

7. What will people be saying about youth? About the government? About the possibility of war? About recreation?

8. What will be a major problem in society at that time?

9. What will be the greatest invention at that time?

10. What will grocery shopping be like?

11. Will the energy problem be solved? If so, how?

12. What is your feeling about the next 20 years?

After having shared this letter with your friends, seal the letter in an envelope, address it to yourself, and give it to someone to mail to you 20 years from now. Who do you know that will know where you live 20 years from now.

FOCUS: To provide students the opportunity to speculate on the impact an innovative luxury has on society.

TARGET: Discovering, Cooperating, Communicating

BLAST OFF: A solar-powered talking watch that not only literally "tells" the time but also nags you awake with alarm messages such as "time to get up, go, go, go" will be marketed soon by the Windert Watch Company of Los Angeles. Available in four languages, the talking watch will also have a snooze control warning "you are now ten minutes past your alarm time." The watch will retail for less than $100. It seems as if the appearance of Dick Tracy watches with TV screens and voice transmitters are just around the corner. Using the Impact Inventory Form on the student activity page, determine with the class as a whole, the first line consequences that a talking watch might have on our lives. For example, one consequence would be that there would be fewer alarm clock sales. Once the first line consequences have been determined, have the class cite the second line consequences resulting from the first line. For example, because there would be fewer alarm clock sales, alarm clock manufacturers might lose their jobs. Having completed these two steps, come to some general conclusion about the desirability of talking watches. Remember that this is to be a group exercise. Students will need to be reminded how a group can most effectively communicate (e.g., wait until the other person is finished before talking, bear in mind that others may wish to talk, keep on the topic being discussed, etc.) A circle grouping pattern is the most desirable.

Variation: Choose a different innovation and complete the same exercise (e.g., a TV watch).

19

THE TALKING WATCH

What would be the consequences if most people owned a talking watch. Fill in the boxes.

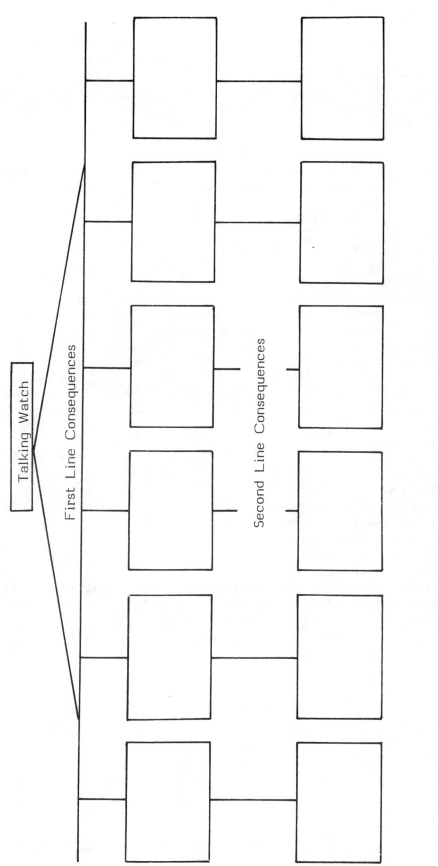

Talking Watch

First Line Consequences

Second Line Consequences

Conclusions about the desirability of a talking watch.

_____

_____

_____

Would you buy one? yes _____ no _____

FOCUS: The primary purpose of this activity is (a) introduce students to the future, (b) provide for an opportunity to forecast future events, and (c) develop their ability to think positively about the future.

TARGET: Creating

BLAST OFF: A simple but meaningful introduction to the future is via the postage stamp. Begin by talking about the intention or purpose of commemorative postage stamps.

Bring in examples of commemorative postage or ask the classroom stamp collector to do so (every class has one). Help students begin thinking about possible future historic events and eventually get down to the task of having the students design their own stamps. One point that should not be overlooked is that commemorative stamps commemorate an event or person that is something positive and/or has improved society. Once completed, have drawings laminated and make a classroom scrapbook to use as a resource in a future learning center to show visitors.

THE "SAVANNAH"
The first steamship that crossed the Atlantic

MY POSTAGE STAMP OF THE FUTURE

FOCUS: To provide students the opportunity to take pride in themselves and in their school.

TARGET: Valuing, Cooperating

BLAST OFF: Kino Learning Center, an elementary school in Tucson, Arizona, adopted the slogan "Kino Kids Care." The objective being to increase students' pride in their school, in themselves, and in their teachers. Students developing this "we" feeling can do much to eliminate moral and discipline problems in a school. Completing the exercise on the student activity page could be a first step to begin helping students develop or reinforcing pride in their school. This should be done as a group, getting as many ideas as can be generated, accepting the ideas of others, and providing all to have input are some of the cooperation skills to be remembered.

Variation: Spin off from this exercise could include having buttons or banners made for the school with monies going for a special take pride in our school night. A thermometer chart could be kept to record monies taken in to reach a predetermined goal.

A. What three things do kids and teachers value most?

B. What are things we do at our school to show we have a "we" feeling?

C. What word best describes our school?

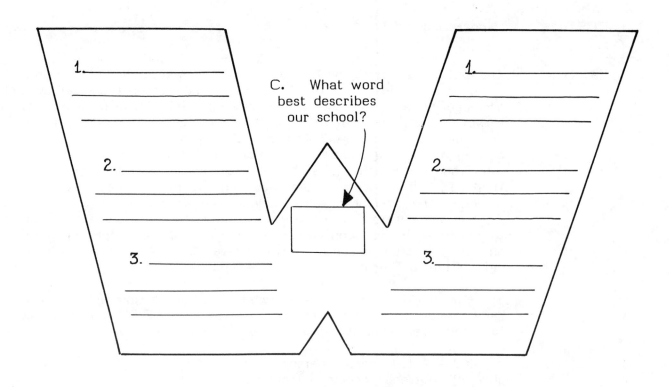

1. _____
   _____
   _____

2. _____
   _____
   _____

3. _____
   _____
   _____

1. _____
   _____
   _____

2. _____
   _____
   _____

3. _____
   _____

D. If we were to design a flag for our school, what would it look like?

E. What two things do you value about the teachers in your school?

1. _____

2. _____

F. Why should future kids in this school remember the students now in this school?

COUNT DOWN: Am I a People Person   # 22

FOCUS: To provide the opportunity for students to self-evaluate their own
                progress and/or potential for getting along with people.

TARGET: Cooperating

BLAST OFF: The better teachers know their students, fewer disciplines will result.
                In addition, if kids come to know one another, respect one another,
                and can work with others, discipline problems will be lessened.
                However, the purpose of this activity is not for solving the discipline
                dilemma but to help students assess their progress and potential for
                getting along with people.   Students learning how to cooperatively
                work together is something that should occur throughout the school
                year.   To help students become aware of its importance, have them
                complete the student activity page.   The items can be used as a
                personal self-awareness instrument and/or it can be used as a vehicle
                to conduct individual conferences with students.   You could complete
                one for each student and then compare results with what the student
                did for him or herself.

                The students can get an idea of where they are at in being a people
                person by adding numbers circled and dividing by 12. Using the chart
                to categorize themselves will indicate amount of growth needed.

                50 - 60 - A true people person
                40 - 49 - Often a people person
                30 - 39 - Sometimes a people person
                20 - 29 - Seldom a people person
                 1 - 19 - A person

WHIPPING-POST

22

AM I A PEOPLE PERSON

How do you rate yourself in each of the following questions: Circle the number which best fits you.

		Yes				No
1.	Do I help my classmates when they ask me?	5	4	3	2	1
2.	Do I let my classmates know I like them?	5	4	3	2	1
3.	Do I live up to my agreements with them?	5	4	3	2	1
4.	Do I work well with my classmates when we have a group activity?	5	4	3	2	1
5.	Do I help others follow the classroom rules?	5	4	3	2	1
6.	Do I avoid saying unkind things about my classmates?	5	4	3	2	1
7.	Do I feel good about myself in school?	5	4	3	2	1
8.	Do I share some of my problems with my classmates or teacher?	5	4	3	2	1
9.	Do I allow my classmates to say what they think or feel?	5	4	3	2	1
10.	Do I accept my classmates as people who may be different from myself in some ways?	5	4	3	2	1
11.	Do I control myself and adjust my behavior in an acceptable way?	5	4	3	2	1
12.	Do I continually seek to improve myself in getting along with others?	5	4	3	2	1

From the above ratings I learned that I _____

_____

_____

One thing I am proud of is _____

_____

_____

One thing I can improve on is _____

_____

_____

COUNT DOWN: Taking Time Today   **#23**

FOCUS: To provide students the opportunity to become responsible for using their time wisely.

TARGET: Communicating

BLAST OFF: Learning how to use one's time wisely is an important skill that can and needs to be learned. There are things teachers can do to enhance learning in this area. Certainly, with the pace of life accelerating, being concerned about using time wisely is of increasing importance. Begin by discussing ways in which we waste time at home and at school. Have the students guess how many minutes they waste in school in a day and then multiply this by five to get a weekly average. Pose the question, "what could you do that would be a better use for this time?" Using the student activity page, have students circle one or two items they would like to concentrate on for two weeks. Each morning they are to take out a sheet and place a check along side the circled item(s) chosen if they did do that the day before. A quick stroll down each aisle to see how each student is doing will be a reminder to them to take it seriously. Putting the papers in a special booklet is important and giving them a special award at the end of the two weeks are positive reinforcers.

NOTE:
The editor does recognize
the sexism on this page,
but that's the way it was
in 1921.

TAKING TIME TODAY TO . . .

During the next two weeks I am going to use my time better by (circle one or two):

Days
1 2 3 4 5 6 7 8 9 10

1.   being ready to do my work

2.   not bothering my classmates when
     they are working

3.   not interrupting others

4.   listening to my teacher

5.   getting to school on time

6.   cleaning up the room

7.   not daydreaming

8.   working when the teacher leaves
     the room

9.   visiting with a different person
     each day

10. asking questions when I don't
     understand something

11. sharing something with someone
     each day

12. moving quickly to and from class

13. listening to the ideas of others

14. helping my classmates

15. saying hello to other teachers

16. not losing my assignments

17. watching 1/2 hour less of TV

18. talking with my parents about
     what I am doing in school

19. doing my best not to waste time

20. completing my work on time

Are you spending too much time on hold?

COUNT DOWN: It's the Same, It's Different

FOCUS: In helping the students understand change as well as stability, this activity will provide the opportunity to determine the similarities and differences occurring between the past, present, and the future.

TARGET: Choosing

BLAST OFF: In studying the past, one is quick to note the differences between then and now. Few, however, take time to note the similarities. This is especially important to help young people maintain a sense of stability. Using the student activity page, begin by having students cite the differences between now and 20 years ago. Also note the similarities. Having done this, have students predict what similarities will occur between now that the year 2000. Also cite the differences. Conclude the discussion by having students cite what things they would like to remain the same. Use the past, if possible, to determine if a similar idea, invention, etc., remained the same.

Variation: Discuss the similarities and differences existing between now and one year ago. Do the same thing one year from now.

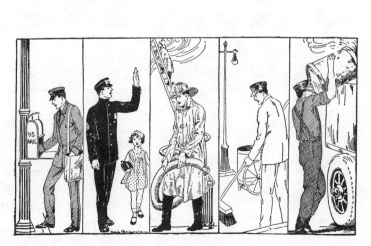

24
IT'S THE SAME, IT'S DIFFERENT

The past _____
            Date

The present _____
               Date

Differences

_____

_____

_____

_____

Similarities

_____

_____

_____

_____

The Present _____
               Date

The Future _____
              Date

Differences

_____

_____

_____

_____

Similarities

_____

_____

_____

_____

The things I would like to remain the same are:

1. _____

2. _____

3. _____

Women in the Armed Forces

TOMORROW'S FUELS

The Unisex Look

FOCUS: To help students decide alternative solutions to problems when the best solution is not available.

TARGET: Choosing

BLAST OFF: Many of us know the best answer to a problem, but seldom do we think of an alternative if the best is not available. Raising this question may have quickened the solution to the energy problem if we would have focused on the best of the remaining alternatives years before it became a problem. To help students decide "the best of the rest", have them respond to the questions on the activity page, discuss in large or small groups, and then have them generate their own problems with potential alternative solutions. This is a good exercise for helping students develop analytical thinking required in mathematics.

THE NEIGHBORHOOD USING THE SCHOOL BUILDING

Sometimes the best answer to a problem is not always available. When this happens, you have to look at the rest of the answers. Read the problem under "The Best" column and write your answer in "The Rest" commmn.

THE BEST	THE REST
There are no water color paints in the house to paint a picture on paper. What else could you use?	
The net you use to catch butterflies has a big hole. What else could you use?	
You are picking up sea shells and you have no sack to put them in, what else could you use?	
The fishing line is too long, no knife is available, what can you use to cut it?	
Your bicycle fender is bent, no hammer is available to fix it. what else could you use?	
You want to leave a note to your parents, no paper and pencil is around, what else could you use.?	

Think of three other problems like the ones above and write them below.

The Best	The Rest

FOCUS: To provide students the opportunity to use creative thinking and imagining skills in visualizing a science fiction world of the future.

TARGET: Creating

BLAST OFF: Science fiction has long been a tool for visualizing future worlds. In spite of its seemingly "out of focus" view of events, many science fiction worlds described in the science fiction writings of yesterday have become realities. Thus, using science fiction writings as a tool to help youth visualize the future has been a popular strategy utilized by many teachers in futurizing their classrooms. You may wish to introduce this activity by reading a science fiction story to the class and follow it up with these kinds of questions:

1.   When did the story take place (i.e. what year)?

2.   Was it a positive or negative view of the future?

3.   What is the likelihood of the events in the story actually occurring?

4.   What new discoveries were used in the story which do not exist today?

5.   Did the people in the story act any differently than people do today (i.e., are there different customs)?

6.   Is there evidence of some government in the society?

Having discussed the story with the students, the next step is to have the students do some "sci-fiing" by having them write their own science fiction story. The student activity page can serve as a cover for their story as well as an aid in helping them imagine the future world they will be writing about.

SCI - FIING

My story title _____

Year in which my story takes place _____

New inventions or discoveries used in my story

_____

_____

_____

Where my story takes place _____

Names of people in my story _____

_____

_____

My story is an _____ optimistic or a _____ pessimistic view of the future (check one).

I believe my story _____ will happen, _____ will not happen, _____ might happen (check one).

THE 85 M.P.H. TREES

FOCUS:

The primary purpose of "trending" is to help students become aware of current trends to determine their full meaning upon their lives now and in the future.

TARGET:

Choosing

BLAST OFF:

To begin, discuss with students what is a trend. An early way to identify a trend is "something that is decreasing or increasing over a period of time." Brainstorm trends with students (e.g., more smaller cars, more time for recreation, more working mothers, etc.) If students have trouble identifying trends, mention some items and have students analyze whether or not it is a trend. For example, "Is smoking on the increase or decrease?" "People are buying more than one TV for their homes." Is this a trend? Once having identified some trends, have students put them on the accompanying "Trending Grid" for further analysis. Pay particular attention to how trends affect their lives and the students' forecast of their duration.

Variation: Have students bring in articles depicting trends and devote 10 minutes of every day or class period discussing the trend and its implications. In addition, have an on-going classroom bulletin board or classroom scrapbook depicting trends. This makes an excellent up-to-date social studies resource book. Zeroing in on science and math trends only is an easy way to integrate this activity.

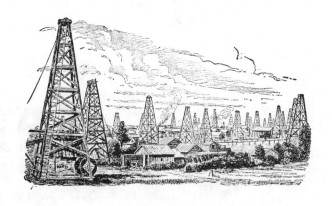

TRENDS THAT SHAPE THE FUTURE

27
TRENDING

1. Identify some trends (things that are increasing or decreasing) and list them in the "trends" column.
2. In the second column, identify who these trends will affect (e.g., myself, young people, old people, men, women, only people in your town, everyone, etc.). Also, briefly state how the trend will affect these people.
3. In the third column, identify one advantage of the trend.
4. In the fourth column, identify one disadvantage.
5. In the fifth column, forecast how long you believe the trend will last (e.g., one month, 6 months, one year, 10 years, etc.)

(1)	(2)	(3)	(4)	(5)

FOCUS: To provide students with the opportunity to express their feelings about how they see themselves in the future, to brainstorm solutions to some future problems, and to give each student some positive feedback.

TARGET: Communicating

BLAST OFF: This is an excellent activity illustrating that the process is equally as important as the product. Divide class in groups of 6-8 students. Pro-vide each member with a student activity page.   In each group, students are to take turns describing a success they will experience sometime in the future. In addition, each student is to identify a problem that society will face sometime in the future. You may want to have students focus on a long range future (i.e. 10-20 years from now.) While a student is identifying his/her success as well as the societal problem, the other students in the group should be identifying a strength of this particular person, (e.g., outgoing, determined, enjoys life, etc.) The success, the problem, and the strength should be noted on the activity page. When a student is finished, the other members in the group read off the strengths of that particular person.

After all students have been given an opportunity to speak, the individual groups are to focus on the societal problems to determine if any of their future successes will be influenced by societal problems (i.e., they are to put themselves in the future). A large group summary session can follow with these kinds of questions being asked.

1.   Was there a similarity of societal problems? (Put some of these problems on the board).

2.   Was there a similarity of future successes?

3.   Are any of the societal problems insurmountable?   Is there anything we can do to help solve any of them now?

4.   How did you feel about your strengths.   Were there some surprises?

Comment: Whether or not members of the group know one another is not that critical. What is important is that students are able to identify some strengths in all people.

28
SEEING MYSELF IN THE FUTURE

You will be spending your life in the future, have you thought about your life in the future? What successes will you have? What problems will society face? What are some of your strengths that will test your ability to cope with some of these problems? Completing the chart below will help you answer some of these important questions. In your group, write down the member's name in column I. Follow the directions of your teacher in completing the remaining three columns.

Column I NAME	Column II HIS/HER FUTURE SUCCESS	Column III A SOCIETAL PROBLEM	Column IV HIS/HER SRENGTHS

The World will change a great deal by the year 2076.

(...and so will you.)

FOCUS: The purpose of this activity is (a) to provide students with an opportunity to experience a probable future, (b) to help students empathize with various members of society, and (c) to increase their communication, persuasive skills.

TARGET: Communicating, Cooperating

BLAST OFF: Class members are divided in groups of 5 or 6. Each person receives a 3 x 5 card describing the role he/she will play. One of the people in the group is designated as group leader. Possible roles could be the following: 1) clergyman - large congregation, two years away from retirement; 2) senior citizen - has trouble speaking English, cannot drive very well, likes to visit friends in neighboring town; 3) social worker - working mother; 4) salesman - successful, drives Cadillac; 5) housewife - 2 children in school, divorced, no job; 6) high school English teacher - single, likes weekends for recreational pursuits. The leader begins by having each person describe their needs and uses activity sheet to record needs (members of group may wish to do so also). They can add to their stories to make them more persuasive, but they must give all information stated on the cards. The leader has been given 14 coupons to distribute to his/her group. Each coupon is worth 5 gallons and is good for one week. A person may receive from 0-4 coupons. The leader makes the final decision, he/she uses any method to arrive at this decision (e.g., unilateral, concensus, voting, etc.). Once the activity is completed, these questions should be posed to the group: 1) how did the leader arrive at his/her decision? 2) Did all members of group have equal opportunity to discuss their needs? How was this facilitated? 3) Compare the number of coupons awarded to a member in one group to some person in another group. If they are different, what argument was used to obtain more coupons? 4) What is the likelihood of rationing occurring? Has it occurred at other times in our society?

GAS RATIONING BEGINS TODAY

PERSON	NEEDS DESCRIPTION	NO. OF COUPONS AWARDED
1.		
2.		
3.		
4.		
5.		
6.		

1 coupon = 5 gallons (good for one week)   14

FOCUS: The primary purpose of this activity is to allow students the opportunity to speculate on careers of the future.

TARGET: Discovering

BLAST OFF: Changes in society due to technological growth, discoveries, progress, etc. will bring about different types of employment possibilities. To provide students with an idea as to how new jobs develop resulting from the invention of the auto, television, or the outboard motor. Tell the students that their task is to create some job openings that might appear in the want ads of a 1996 newspaper due to changes in society between now and then. Review current want ads to get an idea as to how they are composed. Once written, have students decide which ones are most likely to occur. Share want ads with rest of class. After doing this, read some of the want ads on this page and discuss their likelihood of occurrence.

Variation: Have students identify future jobs related to math and science fields.

DIRECTIONS: In the boxes located below, describe some job openings
that you think might appear in the want ads of a 1996 newspaper. To
get an idea of what is written in a want ad, review the various want
ads located on this page. Considering those which you have written,
which ones are you most certain will occur? Place an "X" in the upper
right hand corner of these boxes.

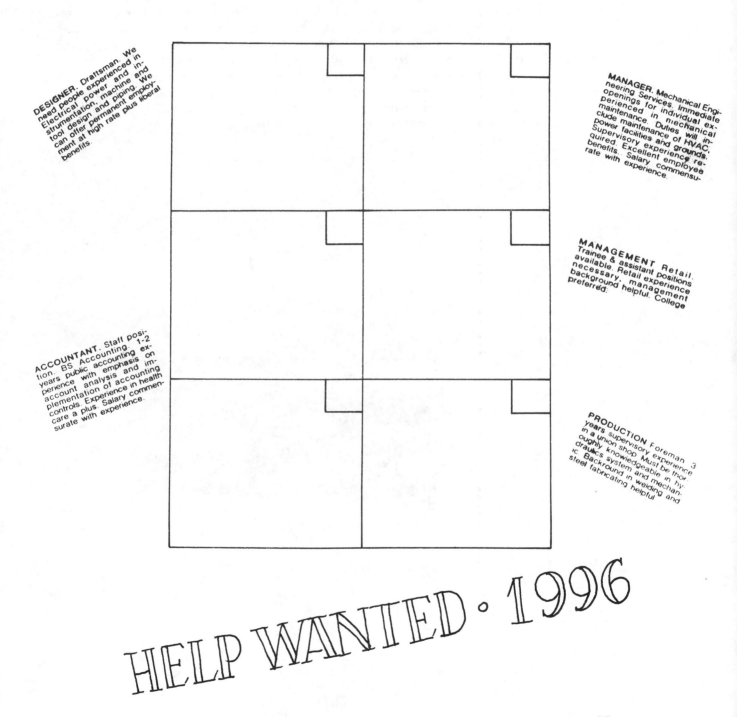

DESIGNER. Draftsman. We need people experienced in Electrical power and instrumentation, machine and tool design and piping. We can offer permanent employment at high rate plus liberal benefits.

MANAGER. Mechanical Engineering Services. Immediate openings for individual experienced in mechanical maintenance. Duties will include maintenance of HVAC, power facilities and grounds. Supervisory experience required. Excellent employee benefits. Salary commensurate with experience.

ACCOUNTANT. Staff position. BS Accounting. 1-2 years public accounting experience with emphasis on account analysis and implementation of accounting controls. Experience in health care a plus. Salary commensurate with experience.

MANAGEMENT Retail. Trainee & assistant positions available. Retail experience necessary, management background helpful. College preferred.

PRODUCTION Foreman 3 years supervisory experience in a union shop. Must be thoroughly knowledgeable in hydraulics system and mechanic. Backround in welding and steel fabricating helpful

HELP WANTED ∘ 1996

FOCUS: To help students have a greater awareness of the reality of future shock.

TARGET: Discovering

BLAST OFF: Begin by talking with students about what it is to experience culture shock.   Perhaps some students have been to a different country. Whereas culture shock occurs when one cannot cope with the many changes an outsider feels when traveling to another culture, future shock can occur without doing any traveling whatsoever.   It results when people experience too much change in a short period of time. Recent examples of signs of possible future shock are lines at gasoline stations, nuclear energy mishaps, air pollution, etc.   Having discussed this term with the students, complete as a group the student activity page.

31
BEWARE! MY NAME IS

Hi! You can just call me future shock. I live just around the corner.
At one time I was seldom thought about but recently I have been given
more and more attention. In case we should run into one another, this
is how you can recognize me:

1.   Recent signs of my presence are

2.   You can destroy me by

3.   I grow stronger when

4.   The word(s) that best describe me is

5.   I don't like people who

6.   Something I enjoy doing is

7.   A good friend of mine is

8.   If you were to draw something to symbolize me, it would be

Shock Treatment

COUNT DOWN: Ten Actions for Peace   #32

FOCUS: Helping students feel that they can make a difference in creating a
                more peaceful world.

TARGET: Creating

BLAST OFF: One often wonders whether or not we will witness the year 2000.
                Some feel that if we keep our present course, no one will see it. On
                the other hand, if changes can occur, we can truly have a bigger and
                better world.   Located on the student activity page are various
                options your students can choose to initiate some positive action
                towards our becoming a world of peace.   The students are to check
                the one they intend to carry out and sign their name at the bottom.
                This represents a learning contract. Follow this up by setting aside
                10-30 minutes a week for "Time for Peace."

                Variation: You may wish the entire class to participate in one peace
                activity before providing the other options.

32

Check the Action for Peace activity you wish to do; sign your name and date at the bottom, and begin to build for peace by carrying out the activity.

1. Find out what peace organizations are doing by writing to: Institute for World Order, 1140 Avenue of the Americas, New York, NY 10036.	2. Identify 10 things the world could do to bring about peace.	3. Check your library to discover what materials on war/peace are available. Which kind do they have more of, war or peace?
4. Write your local editor on war and peace issues that interest you.	5. Write to your elected and appointed officials. Let them know where you stand on peace.	6. Participate on a panel to talk about ways to revers the arms race, or other peace related topics.
7. Start your own program- think of a new way to reach people for peace. Identify the first 3 things to achieve your goal.	8. Identify 10 things currently being done on a local, national, or international level that are positive steps toward peace.	9. Get involved by encouraging war prevention studies in your school and make a point to talk with at least 3 teachers about what they are doing.
10. Make a poster or bumper sticker e.g. "I want to see the year 2000" which describes your commitment to peace.	SIGNED _____ DATE _____	

FOCUS: To provide students the opportunity to understand potential impact of computers.

TARGET: Discovering

BLAST OFF: One thing is certain about the future, computers will increasingly play an important part in our lives. Many retail stores now offer home computers for sale at a lesser cost than some color TV sets. If they follow the pattern of the pocket calculator, they will become even more convenient to purchase. Gather what information you can about computers and/or invite someone from your school district who works with computers. The important thing is to give your students some background information about computers. On the student activity page, have the students write a poem about computers using whatever style of poetry you choose. You may wish to read the following poem to the class as an example.

Computers, Computers

Computer science
Computer appliance
Everything a computer.

Even though they're all computers,
They all do look a bit cuter.

No more writing
No more fighting.

Cause if you do
You'll be black and blue

A pill for dinner
A pill for lunch
When will I ever have a regular brunch.

Variation: Select other futuristic topics to have students write poems. Some other topics could be: space flight, laser beams, artificial human organs, ocean farming, synthetic food, intelligence drugs.

MULTIPLICATION TABLE.

1	2	3	4	5	6	7	8	9	10	11	12
2	4										
3	6	9									
4	8	12	16								
5	10	15	20	25							
6	12	18	24	30	36						
7	14	21	28	35	42	49					
8	16	24	32	40	48	56	64				
9	18	27	36	45	54	63	72	81			
10	20	30	40	50	60	70	80	90	100		
11	22	33	44	55	66	77	88	99	110	121	
12	24	36	48	60	72	84	96	108	120	132	144

COMPUTER POEMS

_____

TITLE

_____

_____

_____

_____

_____

_____

_____

_____

_____

HAS THE BIG COMPUTER GOT YOU?

FOCUS: To acquaint students with energy alternatives and some of the advantages and disadvantages of each.

TARGET: Choosing

BLAST OFF: Brainstorm with students the many kinds of alternative energy sources which are available to us. Compare this list with the list below. Have students select 10 sources. For each source listed, students independently write one advantage and one disadvantage. Also have students rank them in order of their potential for solving the energy problem before the year 2000. After each has completed, have students share the advantages, disadvantages, and ranking for each source. During the forthcoming weeks, have students bring in articles relating to the various energy alternatives. Use this information to make composite "Energy Sources" chart for the class. Pass it around to other classes for their use.

Variation: Develop an energy source survey to give to parents.

Coal	Thermo nuclear
Shale Oil	Garbage
Bio-mass	Plasma
Animal	Satellite
Methane	Solar
Alcohol	LP
Diesel	Geo-Thermal
Wood	Natural gas
Wind	Oil
Rivers	Tides

A VIKING SHIP

ENERGY CHOICES: WHAT ARE THEY

Many alternative forms of energy exist. Can you think of ten? What would be one advantage and one disadvantage of each? Also, rank them from 1 (most) to 10 (least) according to the potential you think they have in solving the energy problem before the year 2000.

ENERGY ALTERNATIVE	ADVANTAGE	DISADVANTAGE	RANKING

OIL BONANZA

Growing Energy Under Water

FOCUS: To provide students the opportunity to work together in speculating on what the future may be like.

TARGET: Cooperating

BLAST OFF: Not too long ago, a Japanese World War II soldier was found after having hidden in the Philippine jungles since World War II. In no way did he have communication with the outside world. Wouldn't he be surprised at all of the events and things that make up today's world (e.g., men having walked on the moon, television, air travel, transistor radios, etc.)? Suppose you had been hiding or lost for some twenty years and someone finds you in the year 2000. Have students work with someone they do not regularly associate with in writing a description of life as it will be in 20 years. They might describe what schools are like, what people have in their homes, etc. When finished, discuss what they wrote and also how they felt about working together. Discuss some important things to consider in working with other people (e.g., compromising, willing to share, willing to listen, etc.)

Variation: What five items would the students like to have with them knowing they would not be found for 20 years?

35
LOST FOR 20 YEARS

You have just been found after having been lost for 20 years in a jungle. Decide with your partner what life is like in the year 2000 and write about it in the space below.

_____

_____

_____

_____

_____

_____

_____

_____

_____

_____

_____

_____

_____

_____

_____

Space Life Is Found!

FOCUS: To provide students the opportunity to work cooperatively in fore-casting future inventions, persuading others to believe in their inventions, and to analyze future inventions in terms of their value to society.

WOODEN PLOW, HARROW, AND FORK

TARGET: Cooperating, Valuing

BLAST OFF: Using the student activity page, complete Part I by having students work in small groups to analyze the inventions of the future. Have groups report on their reaction to a particular invention. Next, have each group complete Part II which involves creating their own invention of the future. Completing this part will help them to do Part III which involves "selling" their invention to the rest of the class. Each group is to develop their own commercial to be presented to the rest of the class that would entice others to use this invention.

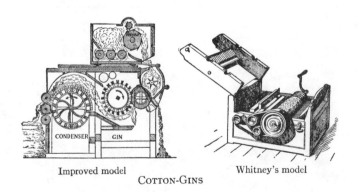

Improved model   Whitney's model

COTTON-GINS

36
INVENTING THE FUTURE

PART I

Determine the value of each invention listed, when you think it will first appear, and some consequences. You may wish to add a couple more.

INVENTION	VALUE HIGH LOW	FIRST APPEARANCE	CONSEQUENCES
1. Artificial Hearts	7 6 5 4 3 2 1		
2. Noice free Motorcycles	7 6 5 4 3 2 1		
3. Robot Mail Delivery	7 6 5 4 3 2 1		
4. 75 Miles per Gallon Autos	7 6 5 4 3 2 1		
5. Pocket Telephones	7 6 5 4 3 2 1		
6. Dome Enclosed Cities	7 6 5 4 3 2 1		
7. Intelligence Pills	7 6 5 4 3 2 1		
8. Computerized Highways (Accident Free)	7 6 5 4 3 2 1		
9.	7 6 5 4 3 2 1		
10.	7 6 5 4 3 2 1		

Can it work?

Part II

Create an invention using the following guidelines.

1) Name _____

2) Purpose _____

3. Advantages _____

4) Disadvantages _____

5) People Served _____

FOCUS: To provide the opportunity for students to realize that their future job choices need not be limited because of their being male or female.

TARGET: Discovering, Choosing

BLAST OFF: In spite of the increasing awareness of non-sexist educational practices and in spite of society's awareness of sexism, one cannot feel confident as yet that students have non-stereotypic attitudes about job choices. Rather, teachers need to continue to emphasize that career choices are not determined by one's sex. Using the student activity page, have students select ten careers of interest to them. In the second column, identify the names of males who have careers in this profession. In the third column, identify females. If students have difficulty in identifying names of males or females in any profession, discuss whether a male or female could fulfill this role and discuss why names of males or females may have been difficult to identify with a certain profession. The point to emphasize throughout the activity is that one's sex should not be a deterrent in choosing careers.

Variation: Keep a class scrapbook of careers and have the students find pictures of both males and females in each career. (The idea for this activity is from Nancy Sweetman, Grant School, Mason City, Iowa.)

A TECHNICAL HIGH SCHOOL WHICH RUNS EVENINGS

In column 1, list 10 careers of interest to you. In column II, name men you know who have careers in the 10 areas listed, and in column III, identify names of women in the same careers. Answer the questions at the bottom of the page when finished.

10 Careers of Interest to me	Men in These Careers	Women in These Careers

In which careers were you unable to identify men who have these jobs?

_____

In which careers were you unable to identify women who have these jobs?

_____

Give some reasons why you were unable to identify men or women or had difficulty in thinking of names. _____

_____

Do you believe being a male or female should be a factor in choosing a specific career? yes_____ no_____. Why or why not? _____

_____

_____

YOUR PERSONAL PLANNING

Women in Politics

COUNT DOWN: Tomorrow's Oscars   **#38**

FOCUS: To provide students the opportunity to cooperatively work together to achieve a concensus and communicate their ideas to others concerning the best of what the future has to offer.

TARGET: Cooperating, Communicating

BLAST OFF: Each year Oscars are awarded to the best in motion pictures. Of the many choices that are available, through cooperation and communication, a concensus is arrived at and the best is chosen to win an Oscar. Begin by discussing how awards such as the Oscars are chosen. Next, divide the class into groups of four, distribute the student activity pages, and tell the students they are going to have the opportunity to select Oscars. Only these will be Oscars in many different fields and the date will not be this year, but 2010 (remind the students how old they will be in that year). Each group is to come up with the best idea for awarding an Oscar in each category. Having completed this exercise, members of the group are to share in the explanation of each Oscar awarded so that other members in the class may understand. Once all the lists have been shared, a composite list could be formed in the form of a boting ballot and distributed to other classes to select the best of the best.

Each year awards (Oscars) are given to the best in movies. If Oscars were given to ward the best the future had to offer, what would they be? The year is 2010.

BEST INVENTION _____

BEST MIRACLE DRUG _____

BEST PEACE PLAN _____

BEST ENERGY SAVER _____

BEST TRANSPORTATION _____

BEST BOOK TITLE _____

BEST MOVIE _____

BEST SONG TITLE _____

BEST WEAPON _____

BEST SPACE ADVENTURE _____

BEST TV PROGRAM _____

BEST CONSERVATION IDEA _____

BEST HEALTH PLAN _____

BEST POLLUTION SAVER _____

BEST NUTRITIOUS FOOD _____

AND THE WINNER IS . . .

IN SEARCH OF

FOCUS: To provide students the opportunity to decide what things they currently value most in life and make some determination as to whether or not these things will be available in the future.

TARGET: Valuing, Choosing

BLAST OFF: Youth making some determination as to what they cherish in life is an important exercise. It is important because this decision making process will determine in many respects, the kind of future in which they will be living. Using the activity page, have the students identify an object, (person, place or thing) which they value most and which corresponds to the word. The next column asks them to make a determination as to whether or not they believe this valued thing will be around in the future. In the bottom half of the page, complete the same exercises in groups of 3-5. Each group is to agree on the valued object for each word given. It is a good idea to review the words with the students before proceeding. You may want to select one and you provide an example of what you would choose. In the discussion that follows, mention not only what each group came up with but also how each group functioned. Ask how the students felt about things that would not be around in the future. How many of the things that would not be around did they have some control over?

39
NOW AND FOREVER

In column 2, identify an object (person, place or thing) which you value most and which corresponds to the word in column 1. For example, if the word was "tasty" you might write in "pizza". In column 3, state whether or not you believe this will be around 25 years from now. In the bottom half of the page do the same thing, but as a group.

Individual

	Valued Object	Available in Future	
		Yes	No
Knowledge			
Beauty			
Fun			
Peace			
Love			
Trust			
Excitement			
Security			
Huge			
Challenge			
Strong			

As a Group

Knowledge			
Beauty			
Fun			
Peace			
Love			
Trust			
Excitement			
Security			
Huge			
Challenge			
Strong			

FOCUS: To provide students the opportunity to determine what they value in careers and take steps to further their awareness of a possible future career.

TARGET: Valuing, Choosing

BLAST OFF: Career choices should be a reflection of one's personality interests, and needs. Upon determining what one values in relation to these criteria, at that point one can begin thinking about a specific future career. The first part of the activity page helps students focus on what they value in a career. The second part asks them to select a number of careers that parallel their value system and the third part asks them to reflect upon the long range picture of this career in the future.

40
MY KIND OF JOB

PART I
How important are the listed statements to you in choosing a career?
Place an X on the appropriate blank.

	Great Importance	Some Importance	Limited Importance	No Importance
1. Prestige	_____	_____	_____	_____
2. Results in helping people	_____	_____	_____	_____
3. Much creativity needed	_____	_____	_____	_____
4. Involves much leadership	_____	_____	_____	_____
5. A lot of pressure	_____	_____	_____	_____
6. Traveling	_____	_____	_____	_____
7. Being on my own	_____	_____	_____	_____
8. Making lots of money	_____	_____	_____	_____
9. Living in a large community	_____	_____	_____	_____
10. Working with many people	_____	_____	_____	_____
11. A very different job	_____	_____	_____	_____

Part II
Based on what I checked above, what three careers would be my kind of job?

1. _____ 2. _____ 3. _____

Part III

Will the need for your kind of job be as good as now _____

Not as good_____

About the same_____

FOCUS: To provide students the opportunity to increase their self confidence in speaking to a group by speculating on the things which will be part of every day life 25 years from now but do not exist today.

TARGET: Communicating

BLAST OFF: A number of items which will probably be available to the consumer within the next 25 years which currently do not exist (at least to the knowledge of this author) may include the following:

      a self-chilling beverage container
      fish crackers (crackers fortified with fish protein)
      solar energy stove
      inflatable suspenders (keep children afloat if they fall in water.)
      ultrasonic bath (instead of a golf ball washer, a people washer)
      electric toilet

All of the above have been, to some degree, already invented. They are mentioned in Stephen Rosen's Future Facts (Simon & Schuster). Mentioning these to the students will give them some idea of things to come. Using the student activity page, have each student list and describe inventions that they think will be commonplace 25 years from now. To obtain a well rounded view of the future, categories have been given. If possible, take time to have the kids draw pictures of the items or make models of the items. When this exercise is completed, have each student introduce one or two of their items via the Johny Carson show format. Another student or you can introduce each student by saying "And, here's _____.
An important part of this lesson is to provide students the opportunity to communicate their ideas to the class in a win-win situation. The result will be an enhanced self-confidence for each student. Don't forget the applause sign.

A RAILROAD TRAIN IN 1831

AND HERE'S $\overset{41}{_____}$

What are some things that you believe will be around 25 years from now but do not currently exist? Name the item and describe it under each category.

KITCHEN ITEM

Name _____

Description _____ .

_____

RECREATION ITEM

Name _____

Description _____

_____

EDUCATION ITEM

Name _____

Description _____

_____

SPORTS ITEM

Name _____

Description _____

_____

ENERGY ITEM

Name _____

Description _____

_____

COMMUNICATION ITEM

Name _____

Description _____

_____

ULTRAVISION

COUNT DOWN: Looking into the Future

FOCUS: To provide students the opportunity to forecast the future and become aware of alternative futures.

TARGET: Valuing, Cooperating

BLAST OFF: Few people are aware of or take seriously the concepts of possible and probable futures. Probable futures represent events almost certain to occur (e.g., increase in world population) and possible futures represent events which may happen but the chances are about 50-50. In both the probable and the possible, an awareness of these events does exist, however, the certainty as to their actually occuring is in doubt. Unforeseen events represent another kind of future where no knowledge of such events occurring currently exists. Examples would be gigantic fires, assasinations, even wars. Probable, possible, and unforeseen represent alternative futures. Using the student activity page, in groups of 4-5, have them list a number of probable futures that they think will happen during the school year in school. Do the same with possible futures, and then, have them brainstorm some unforeseen futures. Have them also check whether the event forecasted is a positive (+) or negative (-) event. At the bottom of the page, have them list a number of events they would like to have happen. Having received all of the ideas from all of the groups for these created futures which represent a fourth type of futures, come to a group concensus as to what they would like to happen during the school year and do whatever necessary to see that it does happen.

42
LOOKING INTO THE FUTURE

WHEN KIDS OF 10 GO OFF TO COLLEGE

Probable Future

Some events that will probably happen this year in school are:

1. _____

2. _____

3. _____

Possible Future

Some events that could happen this year in school are:

1. _____

2. _____

3. _____

Unforeseen Future

Some events which are unforeseen that no one really knows about are:

1. _____

2. _____

3. _____

Created Future

Some events which we would like to happen this school year are:

1. _____

2. _____

3. _____

To the left of each number, place a plus (+) if you think this future event is good and a minus (-) if you think the future is bad.

TICKET TO SPACE

COUNT DOWN: Timeline Mobiles

FOCUS: To provide students the opportunity to chart the significant events in their lives from birth until death.

TARGET: Discovering

BLAST OFF: Having students make a personal timeline is one of the most effective ways of helping students relate to the future. This can serve as a good introduction or culmination to any futures probing. Using the chart on the student activity page, the students are to identify the dates that correspond to significant events occurring in their lives. Because no two lives will have the same significant events, blank spaces are provided to list events specific to an individual. Once they have them listed, have them write these dates and events on individual pieces of cardboard (approximately 3" x 5"), tying them to a coat hanger with string. The mobiles can be made to be more functional by attaching a strip of cardboard 10" from the bottom of the coathanger (see diagram on this page). It could read "John's Timeline: 1974-2062." More events and dates could be hung from the strip of cardboard. Remind students to tie their events to the mobile in chronological order.

Variation: Provide each student a long string stretching from one end of the classroom to another. The students would place their dates and events on the string and hang them between classroom walls.

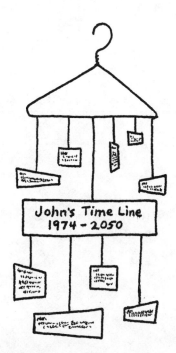

John's Time Line
1974 - 2050

Prior to making the mobile, list the important events that have happened in your life as well as the important events that will happen. For each event, also give the date when you think this will happen. Some events have been provided for you. You will want to put others that apply only to your life.

Event	Date
My birth	
First year in school	
My first time in an airplane	
High school graduation	
The date of my marriage	
My first job	
My retirement	
My death	

My CRYSTAL BALL

COUNT DOWN: Space in Your Mind

FOCUS: To provide students the opportunity to deal with problems confronting space exploration.

TARGET: Creating

BLAST OFF: With the advent of the space shuttle which will, undoubtedly, cause a rebirth in the space program, any type of futuring should include some experiences relating to space technology. The popularity of Star Wars, space age Saturday morning cartoons, songs, TV shows, games, toys, etc. illustrate the interest youth have in space exploration. Unfortunately, much of the information they get is incorrect and distorted. This activity can serve as a good introduction to a unit on space travel, U.S. space program or merely to determine the students' interest in space. Follow up this activity by providing some literature about space travel or space technology and have each student write one question to ask other students.

SPACE IN YOUR MIND

1. When you think of someone landing on the moon, what do you think about?

    _____

    _____

2. Would you like to be an astronaut? Explain.

    _____

    _____

3. What do astronauts and early explorers have in common?

    _____

    _____

4. Should more money be spent in exploring outer space? Why?

    _____

    _____

5. Who should control use of the moon?

    _____

    _____

6. If you discovered a new planet, what would you call it?

    _____

    _____

7. If your class took a field trip to the moon, what would you see?

    _____

    _____

The more you look at it the better it looks.

FOCUS: To provide students the opportunity to understand the major crisis facing the earth and identify possible solutions to such crisis.

TARGET: Choosing

BLAST OFF: Few people realize that a major difference between now and the past is due to the number of crisis affecting planet Earth today. Whereas in the past there were few major problems to resolve, now there are many. In a publication by Champion Internation Corporation (Planting Seeds for the Future) there is a list of a series of these problems. On the student activity page, have the students rank these problems in terms of their seriousness and then under each one, identify one thing they would recommend to solve the problem.

45

<u>A CRISES OF CRISIS</u>

Which world problem do you think is the most serious? Rank them from "1" to "10" with "1" being the most serious. Also, under each one, what answer would you recommend to solve the problem?

Problem	Ranking	Solution
Preventing World War III		
Too many people		
Too few rich and too many poor		
Inflation		
Hunger		
Terrorism		
Energy		
Health costs		
Racism		
Shortage of water		
Young people lack basic skills		
Problems with families		

Reassessing Our Environment

Living With Inflation

PART VI

Creative Encounters Of A " Do It Yourself" Kind:
Futuristic Starter Ideas

The Futures Do-It-Yourself Digest

This part contains a digest of numerous ideas which can serve as a springboard to begin a count down in developing an even larger source of teacher/student activities.

List things people might be willing to give up if they would improve living conditions for the benefit of all people.

Design a recreation area of the future. What might it include? What might it not include that would be included today? Whom would it accomodate? How would it function?

 List things we have today that we didn't have last year, five years ago, or twenty-five years ago. What will we have five years from now that we do not have today?

What might be some popular book titles or television programs in the year 2000.

118

Compute the size of hole it would take to bury all the bags of garbage produced by a school each day, each week, each month. What might they do to have less garbage?

What will the class be like in a 1990 class reunion?

What can you do today that you couldn't do before? What would you like to do in the future that you can't do now? What do you have to do today so that you'll be able to do it in the future?

Design models of future private and public forms of transportation.

Read some science fiction type comic books and talk about those things that could never happen, that might happen, and that will happen.

Write scenarios (a description of a state of affairs at some point in the future and how this condition came about) and discuss their probable consequences.

Survey other students to determine when they think the future is.

Conquer the unknown by figuring out some piece of technology you are unfamiliar with.

Write a biographical sketch about fictitious people tracing their lives for 25 to 50 years into the future.

Plan a model community taking into consideration schools, needs of community, government, recreation, etc. Plan the community for the year 2050.

Explore the viewpoints on the future of parents, teachers, students, etc. Ask them if things will change much in the next 25 years; what they think transportation will be like; if life styles will be different, etc. Use a questionnaire or an interview technique.

Cite personal surprises that affected one's life, discuss the consequences. Will there be surprises in the future? What future events might be most surprising and affect one's life?

List those things that you would like to have 20 years from now to make you most happy. Are the chances good of having these occur?

Develop time lines concerning probable futures and the events that lead up to them. Start from the future and work back. Begin with your own personal life and work back - then with trends.

Imagine you have been lost in the jungle for 20 years. How would you react to today's society? What things would impress you most, the least?

Begin a science fiction story and have the students add a paragraph to the story. Have students write their own science fiction stories.

Posterize your room with pictures depicting possible images of the future. Have a school or classroom poster contest.

Design a structure that will house 100 people and contain all the necessary things in order to survive. It should not be necessary for the people to leave the building. Begin by brainstorming the types of people who would inhabit the building (doctor, educator, economist, etc.) and the things that would be needed.

Redesign your city by drawing a map and placing the various facilities in such a place as to be more convenient, safer, etc. for everyone in the community.

Draw pictures of the interiors of space vehicles. Label or describe what the various dials and gadgets are used for.

Use the students in the classroom or invite students to the classroom who have resided in other communities and have them discuss the advantages and disadvantages of living in that community compared to the community they now live in. What changes would they recommend to improve their present community? What actions can they now take to do so?

Invite a local planning officer in from the community and have him/her talk about those things which must be done before construction of a new building can begin. Discuss the plans which they are undertaking to conserve energy or built-in energy saving devices.

Locate pictures of before and after type urban development projects. What were some of the changes that were made to improve the site?

Read or report about solar energy. Draw what you think to be an efficient solar energy building.

Take a field trip with the primary purpose of looking at ways in which earth is being moved other than by man. What are some ways in which man prevents erosion? Discuss the implication of strip mining on the environment.

Create a totally new environment for the animals in the biology lab.

Create a new interscholastic game which has no losers.

Begin a petition in school for the purpose of having an earth day.

List 10 things relating to technology which were not around 10 years ago. Do you have any of these things in your home which were not around 10 years ago?

Make a scrapbook of futuristic news stories.

Tape the evening news. After each story ask a couple of questions which have futuristic implications.

Make posters relating to various futuristic themes and place them around the school (e.g., population, energy, technology, etc.).

Design your own moon buggy.

Play a number of games which emphasize cooperation between two teams rather than competition.

Write lyrics to a song which you believe typify today's world.

Utilizing a square block of wood, decide how many ways one could use that piece of wood.

Have a Miss Betty Crocker contest. Have students create their own recipes, make them, and invite a panel of judges to sample each food.

Make a graph to show ten largest cities in the world today. Make another graph to show the size of the same cities 25 years ago. Forecast and show on a graph the size of the cities 25 years into the future.

Discuss the kinds of sports activities one can participate in after school; at the age of 30; at the age of 50; at the age of 70.

Talk about the things that would make an ideal community. How many of these things does your community have? Are there any things that you as an individual or class might do to bring about the things your community lacks?

Invite a policeman to talk to the class about changes in crime.

Design a mass transit system. Make models of the vehicles.

Commit yourself to improving the appearance of your school or community. Take before and after pictures.

Write letters to the people in the transportation industry and request that they send you their ideas about future transportation.

List things that are common to you but were not common to your parents when they were your age.

Hooray and Yuk Banners of Today and Tomorrow: students make banners and cut out pictures or write on them things they like or don't like about today's world and the world of the future.

Explore your house and school. List all the objects that would disappear if each of the following ran out: electricity, oil, wood, plastics. Which list is longest? Which is likely to be longest 50 years from now? In which order would you give things up? Why? Survey adults in your community to get their opinions. (Discuss survey.)

A Book About Me: to encourage relating to self, have students make a book of themselves. Pages could include:
a. Title page
b. Pictures of author as baby
c. Pictures of author now
d. Picture of author doing favorite school activity
e. When I am in school, I like to . . .
f. Picture of my favorite animal
g. Picture depicting "I like this best about myself"
h. "Meet my best friend"
i. Myself 20 years from now

Class Yellow Pages of Futurists in Your Community: Compile a classroom version of the yellow pages listing community people knowledgeable in some way of futuristics. Possible categories: people who know something about solar energy, computers, ESP, science fiction, ecology, wildlife management, etc. Share list with other classes.

Have Dictionary, Will Take Ego Trip: provide the class with a list of words that would describe the good characteristics of the students (e.g., jovial, benevolent, bashful, compassionate, gullible, extravagant, etc.). Students are to use the dictionary to find out if the words describe them. Students make a list of the words that describe them and add five more of their own choice.

Tomorrow's society will need a wide variety of new forms to be filled out. Design appropriate forms for the following:
a. ordering a new baby
b. ordering new body parts
c. space travel insurance application
d. application for undersea housing

Make a newspaper or magazine of the future. Humorous? Satirical? Serious? Paper? Microfilm? Tape? TV? What form will it be in? For whom? How often? (Write, construct, design.)

You are what you eat, or so they say. Check through your cupboards at home. Read the lists of ingredients on all the cans and packages. Write down all those you don't recognize. Find out what these things are. What are they for? What do they do? What kinds of foods might you be eating 50 years from now? Write a menu for the year 2025. (Research, write, discuss.)

Construct or sketch a future car (or other vehicle) and demonstrate it to the class. Go for an imaginary ride with a few friends, role playing as you go.

It's 2025 and a particularly nasty air pollutant is beginning to dissolve your house. You've got to get out in one day. Role play your departure. What will you take with you? Leave behind?

You are a business executive trying to make last minute arrangements to get to a meeting on the moon during the height of the Armstrong Day holiday rush. Role play your encounter with the clerk in the travel bureau.

Each student selects one element of the space program (space colonization, astronauts, NASA, moon vehicles, etc.) and completes a project on that topic.

Students draw pictures or design a space travel vehicle.

Have a space food picnic in the classroom.

Students forecast space exploration developments and write reports, draw pictures, or give oral talks on the research.

Debate the pros and cons of space exploration.

Develop a time line of space exploration beginning with the launching of Sputnik.

Design space cities.

"Where Have All the Animals Gone?" Make a list of extinct animals; make another list of animals that are now threatened of becoming extinct; make another list of animals that the students think will become extinct if certain changes aren't made. Discuss the reasons for animals becoming extinct or near extinct. Help them to develop ideas as to what improvements can be made to preserve wildlife.

List the major social problems of the year 1876; discuss how they differ from today's social problems. Brainstorm social problems of the year 2076. Take one or two of these future problems and discuss ways in which it might be prevented. Start at the year 2076 and work backwards until today. Place the things that need to be done on a timeline.

Discuss the problems facing minority groups today in comparison to those of 100 years ago. Discuss those things which have helped bring about some changes. Have students write scenarios about how they feel life will be like for minority groups in the year 2000.

"Grocery Shopping - 2001" Discuss price changes that have occurred within the last 5 years. What food items are less plentiful now, more plentiful? Prepare a list of food items and have the students estimate the cost of the items as it was 25 years ago. Give the list to someone who would be in a position to know the cost of the items and compare the differences. Estimate the cost of the same items in the year 2001. Discuss the reasons for the changes in prices.

Forecast the most popular sports in the year 2000.

Discuss the rate of population growth in the world for the past 100 years. Have the students make charts or graphs depicting its growth. Based on the present growth rates, what will be the population in the year 2000? Make charts showing the life expectancy rate and discuss reasons for increase in longevity.

Make a list of the similarities and differences regarding space exploration and exploration of the earth. What did the explorers have in common? What about the modes of travel, adversities, communication, time, money, etc.? What remains to be explored yet on Earth? In space?

What advancements have taken place with regard to recreational facilities over the past 100 years? With regard to national parks?

Discuss the role of religion over the past 50 years. Forecast its role for the next 25 years. Invite in a clergy to answer questions about the future of the church.

Put on a skit depicting life for city youth 100 years ago. Put on another skit depicting life for city youth 50 years from now.

Interview senior citizens. Get their opinion about how life might be in the future and what they would do to improve life.

Discuss the problems of health as they were 100 years ago and compare them with today's problems.

Re-live the life of a youth 100 years ago for one day. Make a time table which shows what he might be doing every half-hour. Next, do one of yourself showing what you do every half-hour during a particular day.

Debates: Now or the "Good Old Days."

Coping with over-population can be realized by each day restricting class maneuverability (i.e., each day reduce the size of the classroom.

What might the front page headlines of a newspaper read in the year 2000?

Write and act out a 30 second commercial on the latest dehydrated food product (e.g., a tablet size chicken chow mein dinner).

Draw a picture of a robot or a computer type machine with a variety of dials, appendages, and other gadgetry. Have the students discuss individually or in front of a group, the purpose behind each piece of gadgetry and its subsequent effect on their lives -- both positively and negatively.

Create "what if" stories, (e.g., What if there was no longer a threat of nuclear war? What if the Arab nations began another oil embargo? What if I had to walk to school everyday? What if we had solar energy?

Develop maps and charts showing world's main food centers. Develop maps and charts showing world's main population centers. Create a revised world map, graphically depicting the imaginary boundaries and size of nations in relation to their food production capabilities.

Discuss the problems which would arise associated with settling the moon. Decide what types of buildings would be needed to support the people. (Shelter, education, health, job opportunity). Have children draw their own moon city.

Begin by having class brainstorm about recent technological advancement and possible future advancements. Examine how the new vocabulary was created: ASTROTURF. Have students create their own vocabulary for their imagined inventions.

Simulate a space trip into the future making arrangements for supplies such as food, clothing, medicine, etc. that would be needed to establish a new community in the year 2000.

Identify the top 10 achievements in the decade of 1991-2001.

Identify the greatest problems facing families in 1990.

Create an alien language.

Pretend you're a science fiction writer in the 1920's and write a science fiction story taking place in the 1980's.

Develop a restaurant menu as it may appear in 1997.

Futuristic Bulletin Board Ideas

Title: "What is decreasing; what is increasing?"

Description: Have pictures of things which are increasing and decreasing on the bulletin board (e.g., small cars, people, gasoline). Let the students decide which things are increasing or decreasing.

Title: "Automobiles of the Future"

Description: Place drawings made by the students of automobiles of the future on the bulletin board. One constraint would be that each automobile must show one or more improvements over today's autos.

Title: "My Future City"

Description: Have students draw an aerial view of a city which they feel will be typical of cities in the future. Remind them to put in such things as recreational facilities, transportation routes, etc. The only constraint would be that their cities would need to show one or more improvements over today's cities.

Title: "Past, Present, Future"

Description: Put pictures on the bulletin board of things as they were in the past, as they are now, and as they might be in the future. If no pictures of future things can be found, have students draw them. Some examples would be pictures of the students, of ships or of clothes.

Title: "Futuristics in the Comics"

Description: Place covers of comic books which are possible images of the future. Discuss these images with the students. Would they be probable or unprobable, desirable or undesirable? Develop a comic book library or have "a comic book of the week club."

Title: "When is the Future"

Description: Have students take a poll of the students and faculty in the future to get their opinion as to when they think the future is. Put these opinions on the bulletin board in the form of a graph showing what percentage of people think 2000 is the future, 1990 is the future, etc. Break it down into boys and girls, students and faculty, etc.

PART VII

Bonus Encounters Of A Practical Kind:
Duplicate Activity Pages

This part contains a duplicate set of Student Activity Pages that may be detached for photocopying or other means of reproduction.

This provides a means of removing the reproducible pages while keeping the main body of the book intact.

1
ALIEN ENCOUNTER

"Hello, I am an extraterrestial alien. I have a message for you. I have some questions and I have some answers."

Tell Me What You See

My Message:

_____

_____

_____

_____

My Questions:

_____

_____

_____

_____

My Answers:

_____

_____

_____

_____

THE INFORMATION YOU ASKED FOR FROM ?

DISCOVERY!

I found the answer to the energy problem. Here is a picture of my discovery. It is something we see and use every day.

AN ENERGY SAVER

THE ENERGY WAR:
BREW IT YOURSELF

NOW

Date _____

FUTURE

Date _____

4
<u>GETTING AROUND WHEN I'M 21</u>

I am now _____ years old.

The year is _____ . In the year _____ I will be 21.

_____

When I'm 21 this is what I will use to get around in the air.

FLYING SAUCERS

_____

When I'm 21 this is what I will use to get around in the water.

_____

When I'm 21 this is what I will use to get around on land.

The young must try their wings.

_____

CREATURES
OF THE
THIRD PLANET

_____

It's name is_____

6

DIRECTIONS: Write a "What if" question in each box. Answer the question with a drawing. At the bottom of the page write your own "What if" question.

What if _____
_____
_____
_____

What if _____
_____
_____
_____

What if _____
_____
_____
_____

What if _____
_____
_____
_____

My "What if" question: _____

_____

_____

_____

WHAT IF ?

PEACE PILLS
FOR
LEADERS?

The year is 2011. Write a headline for the Society Times newspaper.

The year is 2011. Write a headline about something important that happened to you this year for the My Times newspaper.

8
MY A+ WORLD

1. It is called _____

2. Its symbol is _____

3. Three important laws are:

    _____

    _____

    _____

    _____

4. Two characteristics of its people are:

    _____

    _____

    _____

    _____

5. Two things which make my world better than the world where I currently live are:

    _____

    _____

    _____

6. The first step that the current world needs to do to become an A+ world is:

    _____

    _____

    _____

9
THE MOST IMPORTANT SPELLING LIST

Can you spell them correctly? Use the guide to study from.

NAMES OF STUDENTS IN CLASS

First Name	Last Name
1.	
2.	
3.	
4.	
5.	
6.	
7.	
8.	
9.	
10.	
11.	
12.	
13.	
14.	
15.	
16.	
17.	
18.	
19.	
20.	
21.	
22.	
23.	
24.	
25.	

Teacher's name

10
THE AUTOMOBILE: GOOD OR BAD

What's your opinion about the automobile? List what you believe to be its strengths and weaknesses.

The Automobile: _____

Strengths	Weaknesses
1.	1.
2.	2.
3.	3.
4.	4.
5.	5.

_____

Identify another invention that has seemingly made life better. Identify the strengths and weaknesses of this invention. In addition, select one weakness and provide one possible solution.

Technological Advancement _____

Strengths	Weaknesses
1.	1.
2.	2.
3.	3.
4.	4.
5.	5.

_____

A solution for weakness No. _____ would be: (Explain)

AUTO-RACING WARS

HOW MUCH SHOULD YOU PAY FOR GAS?

11
Fill In Your Future

Answer the questions by filling in the blank space.

1. In what year will you become a grandparent?_____

2. What will you do on the first day of your retirement?

   _____

3. What will be the title of the best movie of the year in 2001?

   _____

4. What's the first question you will ask your home computer?

   _____

5. A modern house of 2011 will look something like:_____

   _____

   _____

6. The most famous artifact found by archeologists in the year
   2500 will be_____

7. Three new words originated in the year 1988 are_____,

   _____, and_____.

8. The most popular toy parents will buy children twelve years from
   now will be_____

9. When your children are five years old, their favorite TV program
   will be_____

10. My favorite hobby in the year 1993 will be_____

11. My greatest fear for the future is_____

    _____

12. Your parents are looking foward to their future because

    _____

    _____

MORE THAN JUST ONE STEP BEYOND

138

MY STRENGTHS:
TODAY AND TOMORROW

Some of my strengths and good things about myself are:

---- (Fold here when finished) ----

The strengths or good things about this person whose name is at the bottom are:

_____

Some strengths and good things I would like to have are:

NAME_____

NOW EVEN BETTER!

Centering
ON NOW.

Are you living in the past present or future? While it is important to study and remember the past and to study the future, it is equally important that we live in the now. In other words, you need to take advantage of every opportunity to live life to its fullest. There are many things you can do in your community and surrounding area without cost. What are some things you can do merely for the asking?

Free Things To Do In My Community

1. _____	9. _____
2. _____	10. _____
3. _____	11. _____
4. _____	12. _____
5. _____	13. _____
6. _____	14. _____
7. _____	15. _____
8. _____	16. _____

FREE
FREE
free
FREE
FREE

THE FUTURE: A BETTER PLACE TO LIVE

Many things are happening in your community and/or world that are making it a better place to live. Within each area listed below, identify one good thing that is happening.

AREA	SOMETHING GOOD
Transportation	_____
Schools	_____
Cities	_____
Recreation	_____
Senior Citizens	_____
Wild Life	_____
Buildings	_____
Energy	_____
Medicine	_____
Foods	_____

"You've Got to Be Optimistic"

THERE HAS NEVER BEEN A BETTER TIME

15
FINDING AND AUCTIONING MY FEELINGS

In column 1, list as many different types of feelings as you can think of. In column 2, place a check beside those feelings you used this past week, in column 3, place a check beside those feelings you used yesterday, in column 4, a check beside the 3 feelings you valued most, and in column 5, a check beside the 3 feelings you wish you could use more often. For columns 6 and 7, wait for the teacher's directions.

1 Feelings	2 Past Week	3 Yester-day	4 Value Most	5 Wish To Use	6 $	7 Feelings Purchased

MY CLUB FOR TOMORROW

_____

!.   Club name_____

2.   Purpose of club_____

3.   Club slogan for bumper sticker or button is_____

_____

4.   Three things this club will do

A._____

B._____

C._____

5.   Three rules of the club are

A._____

B._____

C._____

6.   Its members shall be_____

_____

7.   The first thing it will do is_____

_____

8.   A reason why our school, community, or country will be better because of this club is_____

_____

_____

_____

ENERGY:TOGETHERNESS

PEOPLE PROBLEMS

A young president of a small underdeveloped island nation is faced with a tough decision. He must decide whether or not to allow doctors to vaccinate the entire population against diseases that cause most of the deaths on the island.

At first, this seems like no problem at all and many would even call it a blessing. Other nearby islands vaccinated their population and it cut the death rate in half almost overnight. The result was that twice as many babies lived (for here is where cuts in death rate have the greatest effect). However, the per person food supply dropped sharply on the already near-starving islands.

The president realizes that better health can be spread widely in his country. However, there may be no increases in better schools and more jobs. In fact, employment may fall to a lower level than before. He knows also that starving people do not starve quietly, particularly those people who have "seen it better."

The president feels it is very possible that his young country will not be able to bear the population increase. But he also knows that, when given a choice between life or death, all people -- throughout history -- choose life over death. If his own people hear that he has decided to keep vaccination from their country, it could very well mean death for him.

Three things the president could do are:

1._____

2._____

3._____

If I were president, I would choose No._____

My reasons are:_____

_____

_____

_____

_____

An Impossible Dream?

A LETTER TO MYSELF POSTMARKED 20 YEARS FROM TODAY

Directions: Imagine today's date is 20 years from now. Write a letter to yourself telling about your life at this time. You may wish to use the following questions to guide your writing.

1.   Where will you be living?

2.   Will you be married?

3.   What will you be doing for recreation?

4.   What will your job be like?

5.   What kinds of things will you have in your home that you do not have now?

6.   What kind of transportation will you have?

7.   What will people be saying about youth? About the government? About the possibility of war? About recreation?

8.   What will be a major problem in society at that time?

9.   What will be the greatest invention at that time?

10.   What will grocery shopping be like?

11.   Will the energy problem be solved? If so, how?

12.   What is your feeling about the next 20 years?

After having shared this letter with your friends, seal the letter in an envelope, address it to yourself, and give it to someone to mail to you 20 years from now. Who do you know that will know where you live 20 years from now.

THE TALKING WATCH

What would be the consequences if most people owned a talking watch. Fill in the boxes.

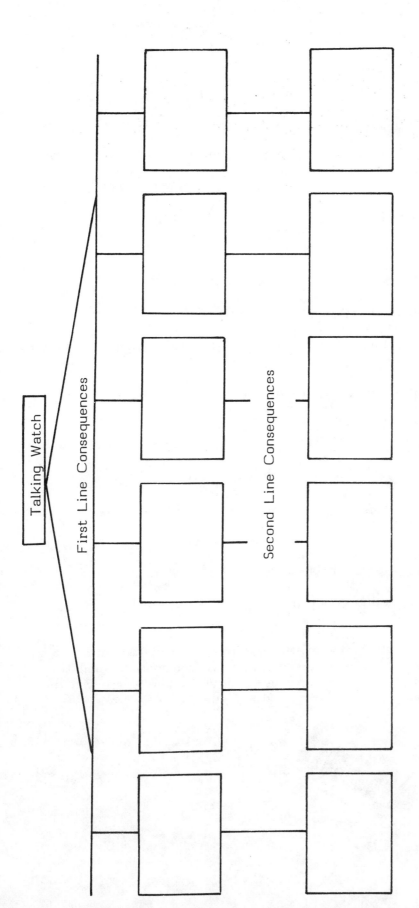

Talking Watch

First Line Consequences

Second Line Consequences

Conclusions about the desirability of a talking watch.

_____

_____

Would you buy one? yes _____ no _____

20

MY
POSTAGE STAMP
OF THE FUTURE

A. What three things do kids and teachers value most?

B. What are things we do at our school to show we have a "we" feeling?

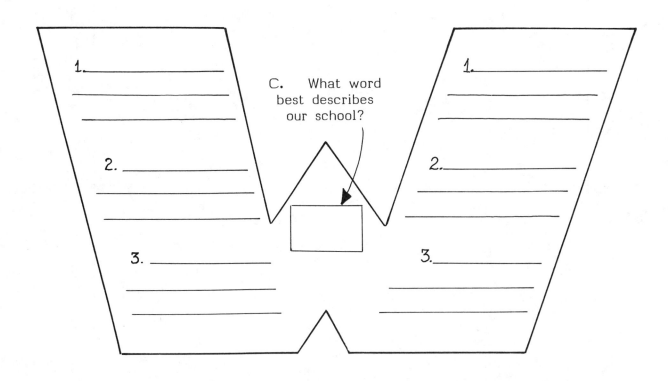

C. What word best describes our school?

1._____
_____
_____

2._____
_____
_____

3._____
_____
_____

1._____
_____
_____

2._____
_____

3._____
_____
_____

D. If we were to design a flag for our school, what would it look like?

E. What two things do you value about the teachers in your school?

1._____

2._____

F. Why should future kids in this school remember the students now in this school?

AM I A PEOPLE PERSON

How do you rate yourself in each of the following questions: Circle the number which best fits you.

		Yes				No
1.	Do I help my classmates when they ask me?	5	4	3	2	1
2.	Do I let my classmates know I like them?	5	4	3	2	1
3.	Do I live up to my agreements with them?	5	4	3	2	1
4.	Do I work well with my classmates when we have a group activity?	5	4	3	2	1
5.	Do I help others follow the classroom rules?	5	4	3	2	1
6.	Do I avoid saying unkind things about my classmates?	5	4	3	2	1
7.	Do I feel good about myself in school?	5	4	3	2	1
8.	Do I share some of my problems with my classmates or teacher?	5	4	3	2	1
9.	Do I allow my classmates to say what they think or feel?	5	4	3	2	1
10.	Do I accept my classmates as people who may be different from myself in some ways?	5	4	3	2	1
11.	Do I control myself and adjust my behavior in an acceptable way?	5	4	3	2	1
12.	Do I continually seek to improve myself in getting along with others?	5	4	3	2	1

From the above ratings I learned that I _____

_____

_____

One thing I am proud of is _____

_____

_____

One thing I can improve on is _____

_____

_____

<u>TAKING TIME TODAY TO . . .</u>

During the <u>next two weeks</u> I am going to use my time better by
(circle one or two):

		Days
		1 2 3 4 5 6 7 8 9 10

1. being ready to do my work

2. not bothering my classmates when
    they are working

3. not interrupting others

4. listening to my teacher

5. getting to school on time

6. cleaning up the room

7. not daydreaming

8. working when the teacher leaves
    the room

9. visiting with a different person
    each day

10. asking questions when I don't
    understand something

11. sharing something with someone
    each day

12. moving quickly to and from class

13. listening to the ideas of others

14. helping my classmates

15. saying hello to other teachers

16. not losing my assignments

17. watching 1/2 hour less of TV

18. talking with my parents about
    what I am doing in school

19. doing my best not to waste time

20. completing my work on time

Are you spending too much time on hold?

IT'S THE SAME, IT'S DIFFERENT

The past _____
            Date

The present _____
              Date

Differences

_____

_____

_____

_____

Similarities

_____

_____

_____

_____

The Present _____
                Date

The Future _____
               Date

Differences

_____

_____

_____

_____

Similarities

_____

_____

_____

_____

The things I would like to remain the same are:

1. _____

2. _____

3. _____

Women in the Armed Forces

TOMORROW'S FUELS

The Unisex Look

25

Sometimes the best answer to a problem is not always available. When this happens, you have to look at the rest of the answers. Read the problem under "The Best" column and write your answer in "The Rest" colummn.

THE BEST	THE REST
There are no water color paints in the house to paint a picture on paper. What else could you use?	
The net you use to catch butterflies has a big hole. What else could you use?	
You are picking up sea shells and you have no sack to put them in, what else could you use?	
The fishing line is too long, no knife is available, what can you use to cut it?	
Your bicycle fender is bent, no hammer is available to fix it. what else could you use?	
You want to leave a note to your parents, no paper and pencil is around, what else could you use.?	

Think of three other problems like the ones above and write them below.

The Best	The Rest

SCI - FIING

My story title _____

Year in which my story takes place _____

New inventions or discoveries used in my story

_____

_____

_____

Where my story takes place _____

Names of people in my story _____

_____

_____

My story is an _____ optimistic or a _____ pessimistic view of the future (check one).

I believe my story _____ will happen, _____ will not happen, _____ might happen (check one).

THE 85 M.P.H. TREES

TRENDS THAT SHAPE THE FUTURE

27

<u>TRENDING</u>

1. Identify some trends (things that are increasing or decreasing) and list them in the "trends" column.
2. In the second column, identify who these trends will affect (e.g., myself, young people, old people, men, women, only people in your town, everyone, etc.). Also, briefly state <u>how</u> the trend will affect these people.
3. In the third column, identify one advantage of the trend.
4. In the fourth column, identify one disadvantage.
5. In the fifth column, forecast how long you believe the trend will last (e.g., one month, 6 months, one year, 10 years, etc.)

(1)	(2)	(3)	(4)	(5)

28
SEEING MYSELF IN THE FUTURE

You will be spending your life in the future, have you thought about your life in the future? What successes will you have? What problems will society face? What are some of your strengths that will test your ability to cope with some of these problems? Completing the chart below will help you answer some of these important questions. In your group, write down the member's name in column I. Follow the directions of your teacher in completing the remaining three columns.

Column I NAME	Column II HIS/HER FUTURE SUCCESS	Column III A SOCIETAL PROBLEM	Column IV HIS/HER SRENGTHS

The World will change a great deal by the year 2076.

(...and so will you.)

GAS RATIONING BEGINS TODAY

PERSON	NEEDS DESCRIPTION	NO. OF COUPONS AWARDED
1.		
2.		
3.		
4.		
5.		
6.		

1 coupon = 5 gallons (good for one week)   14

DIRECTIONS: In the boxes located below, describe some job openings
that you think might appear in the want ads of a 1996 newspaper. To
get an idea of what is written in a want ad, review the various want
ads located on this page. Considering those which you have written,
which ones are you most certain will occur? Place an "X" in the upper
right hand corner of these boxes.

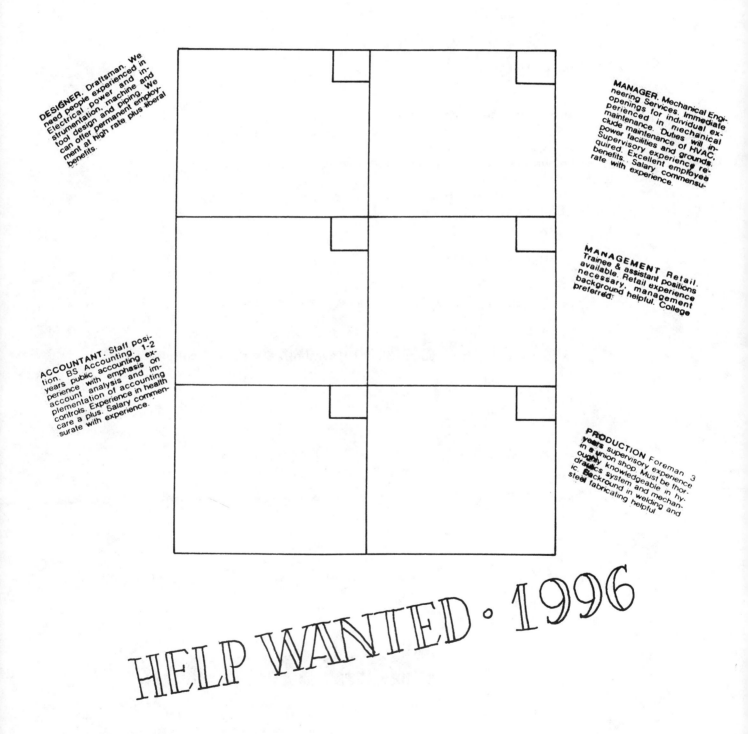

DESIGNER. Draftsman. We
need people experienced in
Electrical, power and in-
strumentation, machine and
tool design and piping. We
can offer permanent employment at high rate plus liberal
benefits.

MANAGER. Mechanical Engi-
neering Services. Immediate
openings for individual experienced in mechanical
maintenance. Duties will include maintenance of HVAC,
power facilities and grounds.
Supervisory experience required. Excellent employee
benefits. Salary commensurate with experience.

MANAGEMENT Retail.
Trainee & assistant positions
available. Retail experience
necessary, management
background helpful. College
preferred.

ACCOUNTANT. Staff posi-
tion. BS Accounting. 1-2
years public accounting experience with emphasis on
account analysis and im-
plementation of accounting
controls. Experience in health
care a plus. Salary commensurate with experience.

PRODUCTION Foreman 3
years supervisory experience
in a union shop. Must be thoroughly knowledgeable in hydraulics system and mechanic. Background in welding and
steel fabricating helpful.

HELP WANTED ∘ 1996

31
BEWARE! MY NAME IS

Hi! You can just call me future shock. I live just around the corner. At one time I was seldom thought about but recently I have been given more and more attention. In case we should run into one another, this is how you can recognize me:

1. Recent signs of my presence are

2. You can destroy me by

3. I grow stronger when

4. The word(s) that best describe me is

5. I don't like people who

6. Something I enjoy doing is

7. A good friend of mine is

8. If you were to draw something to symbolize me, it would be

Shock Treatment

32

Check the Action for Peace activity you wish to do; sign your name and date at the bottom, and begin to build for peace by carrying out the activity.

1. Find out what peace organizations are doing by writing to: Institute for World Order, 1140 Avenue of the Americas, New York, NY 10036.	2. Identify 10 things the world could do to bring about peace.	3. Check your library to discover what materials on war/peace are available. Which kind do they have more of, war or peace?
4. Write your local editor on war and peace issues that interest you.	5. Write to your elected and appointed officials. Let them know where you stand on peace.	6. Participate on a panel to talk about ways to revers the arms race, or other peace related topics.
7. Start your own program—think of a new way to reach people for peace. Identify the first 3 things to achieve your goal.	8. Identify 10 things currently being done on a local, national, or international level that are positive steps toward peace.	9. Get involved by encouraging war prevention studies in your school and make a point to talk with at least 3 teachers about what they are doing.
10. Make a poster or bumper sticker e.g. "I want to see the year 2000" which describes your commitment to peace.	SIGNED_____ DATE_____	

COMPUTER POEMS

_____
                        TITLE

_____

_____

_____

_____

_____

_____

_____

_____

_____

HAS THE
BIG COMPUTER
GOT YOU?

ENERGY CHOICES: WHAT ARE THEY

Many alternative forms of energy exist. Can you think of ten? What would be one advantage and one disadvantage of each? Also, rank them from 1 (most) to 10 (least) according to the potential you think they have in solving the energy problem before the year 2000.

ENERGY ALTERNATIVE	ADVANTAGE	DISADVANTAGE	RANKING

OIL BONANZA

Growing Energy Under Water

You have just been found after having been lost for 20 years in a jungle. Decide with your partner what life is like in the year 2000 and write about it in the space below.

_____

_____

_____

_____

_____

_____

_____

_____

_____

_____

_____

_____

_____

_____

SPACE CITIES

Space Life Is Found!

36
INVENTING THE FUTURE

PART I

Determine the value of each invention listed, when you think it will first appear, and some consequences. You may wish to add a couple more.

INVENTION	VALUE HIGH LOW	FIRST APPEARANCE	CONSEQUENCES
1. Artificial Hearts	7 6 5 4 3 2 1		
2. Noice free Motorcycles	7 6 5 4 3 2 1		
3. Robot Mail Delivery	7 6 5 4 3 2 1		
4. 75 Miles per Gallon Autos	7 6 5 4 3 2 1		
5. Pocket Telephones	7 6 5 4 3 2 1		
6. Dome Enclosed Cities	7 6 5 4 3 2 1		
7. Intelligence Pills	7 6 5 4 3 2 1		
8. Computerized Highways (Accident Free)	7 6 5 4 3 2 1		
9.	7 6 5 4 3 2 1		
10.	7 6 5 4 3 2 1		

Can it work?

Part II

Create an invention using the following guidelines.

1) Name _____

2) Purpose _____

3. Advantages _____

4) Disadvantages _____

5) People Served _____

CAREERS FOR ALL

In column 1, list 10 careers of interest to you. In column II, name men you know who have careers in the 10 areas listed, and in column III, identify names of women in the same careers. Answer the questions at the bottom of the page when finished.

10 Careers of Interest to me	Men in These Careers	Women in These Careers

In which careers were you unable to identify men who have these jobs?

_____

In which careers were you unable to identify women who have these jobs?

_____

Give some reasons why you were unable to identify men or women or had difficulty in thinking of names. _____

_____

Do you believe being a male or female should be a factor in choosing a specific career? yes_____ no_____ . Why or why not? _____

_____

_____

Women in Politics

YOUR PERSONAL PLANNING

Each year awards (Oscars) are given to the best in movies. If Oscars were given to ward the best the future had to offer, what would they be?   The year is 2010.

BEST INVENTION _____

BEST MIRACLE DRUG _____

BEST PEACE PLAN _____

BEST ENERGY SAVER _____

BEST TRANSPORTATION _____

BEST BOOK TITLE _____

BEST MOVIE _____

BEST SONG TITLE _____

BEST WEAPON _____

BEST SPACE ADVENTURE _____

BEST TV PROGRAM _____

BEST CONSERVATION IDEA _____

BEST HEALTH PLAN _____

BEST POLLUTION SAVER _____

BEST NUTRITIOUS FOOD _____

AND THE WINNER IS . . .

IN SEARCH OF

NOW AND FOREVER

In column 2, identify an object (person, place or thing) which you value most and which corresponds to the word in column 1. For example, if the word was "tasty" you might write in "pizza". In column 3, state whether or not you believe this will be around 25 years from now. In the bottom half of the page do the same thing, but as a group.

Individual

	Valued Object	Available in Future	
		Yes	No
Knowledge			
Beauty			
Fun			
Peace			
Love			
Trust			
Excitement			
Security			
Huge			
Challenge			
Strong			

As a Group

Knowledge			
Beauty			
Fun			
Peace			
Love			
Trust			
Excitement			
Security			
Huge			
Challenge			
Strong			

40
MY KIND OF JOB

PART I
How important are the listed statements to you in choosing a career?
Place an X on the appropriate blank.

	Great Importance	Some Importance	Limited Importance	No Importance
1. Prestige	_____	_____	_____	_____
2. Results in helping people	_____	_____	_____	_____
3. Much creativity needed	_____	_____	_____	_____
4. Involves much leadership	_____	_____	_____	_____
5. A lot of pressure	_____	_____	_____	_____
6. Traveling	_____	_____	_____	_____
7. Being on my own	_____	_____	_____	_____
8. Making lots of money	_____	_____	_____	_____
9. Living in a large community	_____	_____	_____	_____
10. Working with many people	_____	_____	_____	_____
11. A very different job	_____	_____	_____	_____

Part II
Based on what I checked above, what three careers would be my kind of job?

1. _____   2. _____   3. _____

Part III

Will the need for your kind of job be as good as now _____

Not as good_____

About the same_____

AND HERE'S _____

What are some things that you believe will be around 25 years from now but do not currently exist? Name the item and describe it under each category.

KITCHEN ITEM

Name _____

Description _____

_____

RECREATION ITEM

Name _____

Description _____

_____

EDUCATION ITEM

Name _____

Description _____

_____

SPORTS ITEM

Name _____

Description _____

_____

ENERGY ITEM

Name _____

Description _____

_____

COMMUNICATION ITEM

Name _____

Description _____

_____

ULTRAVISION

LOOKING INTO THE FUTURE

WHEN KIDS OF 10 GO OFF TO COLLEGE

Probable Future

Some events that will probably happen this year in school are:

1. _____

2. _____

3. _____

Possible Future

Some events that could happen this year in school are:

1. _____

2. _____

3. _____

Unforeseen Future

Some events which are unforeseen that no one really knows about are:

1. _____

2. _____

3. _____

Created Future

Some events which we would like to happen this school year are:

1. _____

2. _____

3. _____

To the left of each number, place a plus (+) if you think this future event is good and a minus (-) if you think the future is bad.

TICKET TO SPACE

Prior to making the mobile, list the important events that have happened in your life as well as the important events that will happen. For each event, also give the date when you think this will happen. Some events have been provided for you. You will want to put others that apply only to your life.

Event	Date
My birth	
First year in school	
My first time in an airplane	
High school graduation	
The date of my marriage	
My first job	
My retirement	
My death	

M y CRYSTAL BALL

SPACE IN YOUR MIND

1. When you think of someone landing on the moon, what do you think about?

    _____

    _____

2. Would you like to be an astronaut? Explain.

    _____

    _____

3. What do astronauts and early explorers have in common?

    _____

    _____

4. Should more money be spent in exploring outer space? Why?

    _____

    _____

5. Who should control use of the moon?

    _____

    _____

6. If you discovered a new planet, what would you call it?

    _____

    _____

7. If your class took a field trip to the moon, what would you see?

    _____

    _____

The more you look at it the better it looks.

A CRISES OF CRISIS

Which world problem do you think is the most serious? Rank them from "1" to "10" with "1" being the most serious.   Also, under each one, what answer would you recommend to solve the problem?

Problem	Ranking	Solution
Preventing World War III		
Too many people		
Too few rich and too many poor		
Inflation		
Hunger		
Terrorism		
Energy		
Health costs		
Racism		
Shortage of water		
Young people lack basic skills		
Problems with families		

Reassessing Our Environment

Living With Inflation